WHO CARES ABOUT THE BIBLE?

WHO CARES ABOUT THE BIBLE?

Where it came from, how to understand it, and why it matters.

by

Tom Hilpert

Nashville, TN

ISBN-13: 978-1535276597
ISBN-10: 1535276592

OTHER BOOKS BY TOM HILPERT

The Lake Superior Mysteries
Superior Justice
Superior Storm
Superior Secrets
Superior Getaway
(more to come)

Non-fiction
In His Image
Who Cares about the Bible?

Fantasy
The Forgotten King

How sweet Your word is to my taste — sweeter than honey in my mouth!
Psalm 119:103 (HCSB)

TABLE OF CONTENTS

PART I: WHERE DID THE BIBLE COME FROM?   9

1: A PERPLEXING BOOK   10

2: A UNIQUE GUIDE FOR HUMAN BEHAVIOR   20

3: ORIGINS OF THE OLD TESTAMENT   29

4: ORIGINS OF THE NEW TESTAMENT   38

5: WHAT ABOUT THE SUPERNATURAL?   55

6: THE MYSTERY   62

PART II: HOW TO UNDERSTAND THE BIBLE   74

7: AN OVERVIEW   75

8: READ THE BIBLE IN CONTEXT   84

9: SCRIPTURE INTERPRETS SCRIPTURE   94

10: GENRE: INTRODUCTION   100

11: GENRE: TEACHING   105

12: GENRE: NARRATIVE   111

13: GENRE: PROPHECY   116

14: GENRE: APOCALYPTIC   122

15: GENRE: PARABLES, PROVERBS, POETRY, SONG   130

16: GENRE: LAWS 137

PART III: ADDITIONAL QUESTIONS 149

17: WHAT DID JESUS SAY? 150

18: VERSIONS AND VERSES 157

19: PRACTICAL TOOLS 162

20: DIFFICULT PASSAGES 170

21: A WONDERFUL BOOK 179

GET INVOLVED 186

ACKNOWLEDGEMENTS 188

ABOUT THE AUTHOR 189

APPENDIX A: THE BASIS FOR MODERN

TRANSLATIONS 190

APPENDIX B: THE KING JAMES VERSION 195

PART I: WHERE DID THE BIBLE COME FROM?

1

A Perplexing Book

The Bible can be an irritating, frustrating and perplexing book.

If you read it much, you can easily find parts that are difficult to understand, or hard to accept. Even if you, personally, *don't* read it very much, in these days of internet-driven social media, you don't have to go far before you are bombarded by people quoting the Bible, misquoting the Bible, contradicting other people who claim they are quoting the Bible, and making things even more confusing, irritating and frustrating.

Some say the Bible contains God's own words. Some say it was made up by the Roman Catholic Church to control people. Some people think the Bible contains a little bit of wisdom and a lot of silly, made-up stuff. Others think there is value in everything in the Bible. Some people think that the Bible does not have much value as a book of history, while others think it does. Some people think it is full of contradictions, while others see ways to harmonize the apparent discrepancies.

If you've spent much time online, you might have noticed some arguments on social media that go like this:

> "Jesus didn't say anything directly about homosexual sex." (This is true).
> "The Bible says homosexual sex is a sin." (This is also true).

Maybe you are familiar with this discussion:

> "The Bible says sex outside of marriage is sinful." (True).
> "The Bible teaches love and forgiveness." (Also true).

Or perhaps you've heard one of these gems:

> "God helps those who help themselves." (Not in the Bible).
> "God never gives you more than you can handle." (Not in the Bible).
> "Everything happens for a reason." (Not in the Bible).
> "Cleanliness is next to godliness." (Again, not in the Bible).

As part of my work, I regularly post blog entries. Someone recently liked my blog, and as I often do, I went over to *his* blog, to check out what he was writing about. I noticed a post with an eye-catching title, and I read it. What I found is similar to many other blogs and social media posts that I have seen over the past few years. The basic argument went something like this:

> ➤ Many Christians claim that, according to the Bible, [enter something here that the Bible says that bothers you, like: "it's a sin to get drunk"].
> ➤ But the Bible also says lots of goofy things, like:
>   - o Rapists can pay their victims' parents 50 shekels, and get off the hook (the writer misquoted Deuteronomy 21, but I think he was referring to chapter 22).
>   - o It's OK to sell daughters into slavery (Exodus 21:7)
>   - o It's OK to marry multiple wives (21:10)
> ➤ Since we don't agree with these goofy things in the Bible, we shouldn't pay attention to what the Bible says about drunkenness [or whatever it is that you don't like about the Bible].

Most commonly, this kind of argument is made in order to justify whatever kind of behavior you like to engage in, while claiming that you follow the Bible. But logically, if that argument was valid (it isn't – more on that later) there would be no reason to pay attention to any part of the Bible at all. If that blogger is right, we ought to just ignore it altogether as irrelevant. If he's correct, we shouldn't pay attention to what the Bible says about Jesus, or forgiveness, or love, either. To be fair, he wasn't saying that in his blog, but it is the logical conclusion.

Now, some of those reading this book may happen to agree with that conclusion. You may think the Bible isn't worth your time or attention. You might think *"Seriously, who cares about the Bible?"* Here's my challenge to you: give me four chapters to get you interested. If you still think the Bible is essentially worthless after reading the first four chapters of this book, well, you gave me a fair hearing, and that's all I can ask.

I suppose, however, that most of the people reading this have some level of interest in the Bible. That's understandable: some of the most cherished values of our culture still come from the Bible. We still appreciate "do not murder." We like the commands about loving our neighbors, forgiving others, and not hating. We like the bits that talk about justice, and those that tell us God loves us and forgives us. If we threw the whole Bible out, we'd be throwing those things out too. Most of those cherished moral values come originally from the Bible. Many of them cannot really be found in other religions. I think you, who have some level of interest in the Bible already, will find this book helpful, and I think you'll even enjoy it.

By the way, I have two useful and reasonable answers to the person who posted the blog entry I mentioned above. I could explain it in about five minutes. But rather than do that, what I want to do is help *you* learn enough about the Bible, and how to understand it, so that you can answer questions like that yourself. You've heard the old proverb: "Give a man a fish, and he'll eat for a day; teach a man to fish, and he'll spend all his nights and weekends in the boat, and his family will never see him anymore."

Actually, I think the second part is "teach a man to fish, *and he'll eat for the rest of his life.*"

I want to teach you to "fish." I could give you the answers to the questions posed by the blog entry I mentioned above. But then, when you encounter new questions, you'll be dependent upon me, or someone like me, to give you answers again. I'd rather help you understand enough so that you can do some digging, and find the answers for yourselves.

It might take a little while. I've been studying the Bible seriously for more than twenty-five years. It won't take you that long to get started and to begin finding answers yourself, but I do hope you look on the Bible as a source that you can, and should, continue to study for the rest of your life. I think that from this book you can learn enough about the Bible to begin.

So, we've briefly considered that the Bible can be confusing. It's a big book, after all. It sometimes appears to teach contradictory things. But there's another side to the story. The truth is, the Bible is a *unique* book.

For one thing, the Bible is the world's most printed book. It is the best-selling book *of all time* – meaning, in the entire history of the world. Not only that, but about half of the population of the whole world derives its religious faith from the pages of the Bible.

Another thing: the Bible is unique in influence. Many of the most wonderful things in the history of the world have come about through the influence of the Bible. I understand if that sounds crazy to you. I won't bore you with too much here, but consider these little things:

- Slavery was abolished because of the influence of the Bible.

- The foundations of modern democracy came from a biblical world view, as well as these ideas: the equality of all people, the right to own personal property, the right to freedom, laws concerning theft, murder and many more.
- Many of the concepts and values that our culture holds dear also come from the Bible: tolerance of those who are different, justice for the poor and oppressed, fairness, caring for those who are needy, love for others and many, many more.
- The whole concept of the University came about because of the influence of the Bible.
- Hospitals were invented because of the Bible.
- Some of the world's greatest art was inspired by the Bible (we're talking Michelangelo and Leonardo Da Vinci).
- Some of the world's greatest literature was inspired by the Bible (we're talking Leo Tolstoy and Fyodor Dostoyevsky).
- Some of the world's greatest music was inspired by the Bible (we're talking Bach and Handel).
- Some of the world's greatest architecture was inspired by the Bible (we're talking cathedrals and basilicas).
- Some of the world's greatest scientists were inspired by the Bible (we're talking Galileo and Isaac Newton).

- Some of the world's greatest philosophers were deeply influenced by the Bible (we're talking Augustine, Aquinas, Kant and Kierkegaard).

Especially in Western culture, much of what has endured through the centuries, and proved itself to be of great worth, sprang either directly from the Bible, or indirectly through the influence of the Bible on society as a whole. That influence spread to the rest of the world, partly through trade, yes, but also because of missionaries who were inspired by the Bible.

Not only that, but the English language, at least, is filled with biblical references, and most English speakers often quote the Bible without even realizing it.

Did you ever find yourself at wit's end? That expression comes from Psalm 107. Maybe you've talked about your broken heart? It was King David who first expressed it that way, also in the psalms. Have you found yourself in a tough situation, and realized that it's just your cross to bear? That saying comes from Jesus, who called his followers to "take up your cross and follow me," (Matthew 16:24).

Here are just a few more:

Bite the dust; cast the first stone; fall from grace; fly in the ointment; forbidden fruit; the powers that be; rise and shine; scapegoat; signs of the times; the straight and narrow; drop in the bucket; wolf in sheep's clothing; writing on the wall.

There are dozens and dozens more. Even when people swear, they are often getting their language from the Bible. (Think about it). For Pete's sake (another), you could go to the ends of the earth (another), in a labor of love (one more), becoming all things to all people (again), and everywhere, you'd find people casting these kinds of pearls before swine (yep).

Sorry, I won't do that anymore. But my point is that, even for those who do not think very much of the Bible, it profoundly influences us, affecting our very language.

Now, let's be honest: the writings of Shakespeare have also greatly influenced modern English. That doesn't mean I have to read all his plays, or change my life just because old Will made Hamlet say, "To be, or not to be." But the information I just shared about the Bible should at least make us pause and say, "This book has been unquestionably influential." It should make it a little harder to simply dismiss it.

So we have this conundrum: the Bible can be frustrating and perplexing. It is often claimed in support of contradicting arguments. At the same time, without question, the Bible has been profoundly and uniquely influential in human history.

When I think about all the confusion surrounding the Bible, I am reminded of the old story about the blind men who went to discover what an elephant was like.

One of the men felt the elephant's trunk, and said, "An elephant is like a snake." Another of the blind seekers found the leg of the great beast, and said, "The elephant is straight and strong like a tree trunk." Another felt the tip of a tusk, and said "an elephant is hard and sharp and pointed, like a spear." Yet one more felt the soft little tuft at the end of the giant animal's tail, and said, "The elephant is soft and furry and small, like a mouse."

WHO CARES ABOUT THE BIBLE?

Here is the thing: all of the men were correct. One part of the elephant *is* like a snake. The elephant's leg *is* like a tree, and so on. What they said was accurate. At the same time, what each one said appeared to contradict the others. How could each one of them be correct?

Let's take this one step further. Suppose you have never seen an elephant, and have only heard the descriptions given by the blind men. It would be tempting to dismiss the elephant as something ridiculous and imaginary. What could be sharp and pointed like a spear, large and rough like a tree, furry and small like a mouse, long and flexible like a snake, all at the same time? It would seem logical to assume that either the blind men are lying, or that they are wildly mistaken.

Of course, if you *have* seen an entire elephant – or even a picture of one – it is quite easy to harmonize the accounts. It is easy, because you have seen the *whole animal*, not just felt one part of it. The elephant is not nearly as weird and improbable as it sounds from the accounts of the blind men.

Many, many people approach the Bible in the same way that the blind men approached the elephant. They see a part of it, and they may even be correct in saying something about one little part of the Bible. But unless you see the whole picture, you have no idea, really, what it is all about. If you relied on the testimonies of those who only have part of the picture, it would be easy to say, "This sounds ridiculous and imaginary." However, like the blind men with the elephant, people can say things about the Bible that are accurate, in a sense, and yet give you entirely the wrong idea.

All of the blind men were technically correct about the elephant. Yet, at the same time, because they did not have the whole picture, they were all also wrong. The same thing happens with the Bible, over and over again.

In this book, I want to show you the whole elephant – the big picture view of the Bible. I think, by the time we are done, you will be able to understand the Bible much more clearly.

THE POINT:

There is a lot of information and misinformation floating around about the Bible. It is a big book, and can be confusing and perplexing. The way that others use, and misuse, the Bible does not make it any easier. Even so, the Bible is one of the world's most unique books, with a distinctive and profoundly positive influence on history. In order to understand it properly, we need to look at the big picture.

2

A Unique Guide for Human Behavior

As I've noted already, I suspect that many people reading this book might already be interested in the Bible; in fact, many of you might already be Christians. But, for this chapter, I want to leave faith out of it, and look at the Bible objectively as a guide for human behavior. I am doing this for two reasons. First, I do hope that some of you readers are honest skeptics who are genuinely looking for more information about the Bible. I think the approach of this chapter might help you. Second, if you are already a person of faith, you can use the information here as you engage in conversations with your friends, family members and coworkers who may be more skeptical than you.

The best place to start, as is often the case, is at the beginning. What *is* the Bible? Where did it come from? Who wrote it, and what is its purpose?

The Bible is not actually one book. It is a *collection* of books. That is one reason why I never recommend starting in Genesis (the first book), and trying to read it straight through all the way to Revelation (the last book). It won't make sense that way, because it isn't that kind of book.

The very earliest parts of the Bible were handed down as oral traditions, and later were written down. Even people with a very rudimentary knowledge of Hebrew (like myself) can see linguistic evidence that much of the first five books of the Bible were originally memorized orally. We'll talk about what that means in a later chapter. The oral traditions, and some new material, were first written down, probably by a man named Moses, sometime around 1400 B.C.

> *By the way, scholars now prefer to note dates as "BCE" and "CE" ("Before Common Era," and "Common Era," respectively). However, the fact is, the "Common Era" begins with the traditional date for the historical birth of Jesus Christ. This means of course, that "Before Common Era" is defined as the time "Before Christ." It seems a little silly to pretend that our modern system of keeping track of years is defined by anything other than the historical life of*

Jesus Christ, because, in actual fact, that is the marker that is used. Whether or not anyone believes in him as anything other than a man, the majority of the world now marks its dates by his historical existence. Changing the designations to BCE and CE does not alter that fact, and seems almost designed to pretend otherwise.
Because of this, I will continue to use BC and AD.

Back to the Bible. More history and more oral tradition were written down by another man, probably the prophet Samuel, sometime around 1000 BC. Samuel also recorded many of the current events of his time. After Samuel, as the monarchy in Israel took shape, court historians kept records of happenings, and further unknown writers recorded more of what we now call the Bible. Prophets spoke, and scribes wrote down what they said. Later, the New Testament was formed from letters and writings of those associated with Jesus Christ.

All in all, the Bible was written by several dozen different people. If you include those who helped to create the oral histories, the number of people who contributed to the Bible is unknown, but it might involve more than a hundred people, or possibly several hundred. It was written in three different languages (Hebrew, Aramaic and Greek). The people who wrote it were from all different walks of life: Farmers, shepherds, kings, court officials, prophets, fisherman, doctors, prisoners, church leaders and more. Some of them were rich, some were poor, and some were in between. The writers came from different cultures, different countries and different continents. There is no sense in which one can say that the Bible was just made up by one person, or even one small group of people at one time. It does not claim that it was dictated in secret by angels.

These facts about the formation of the Bible have never been secret. Scholars have known these things for many centuries. Archeology has consistently confirmed all this. Manuscript study and comparisons also confirm it. These facts are not hidden away somewhere; they are not closely guarded secrets. They are well established.

Now, for comparison, let's look at some other ancient religious writings.

There are some writings that are considered sacred to Hindus, however these are not considered authoritative in the same way that Christians view the Bible, and Hindus disagree about which texts are most important, and even sometimes about which ones are legitimate. The historical origin of the Hindu writings is not well established, nor do the texts claim to be historical in the same way that much of the Bible claims to be. The situation with Buddhism is similar to that of Hinduism. One thing that is helpful to notice about Buddhism, however, is that the core ideas began with just one man (the Buddha). On balance, Hindu and Buddhist texts do not play the same role in those religions as the Bible does in Christianity.

For apples-to-apples comparison with the Bible, we'll consider the Koran, and the book of Mormon – both of which have the same sort of place in their respective religions as the Bible does in Christianity (and, to some extent, Judaism).

The Koran is the holy book which all Muslims accept as the final, authoritative revelation from Allah. Muslims believe it was given to Mohammed in a series of divine revelations in which the angel Gabriel dictated, verbatim, the words of God. The revelations were given over a period of about twenty-three years. They were given only to the prophet Mohammed. Technically, many of the people of the Bible are regarded by Muslims as prophets, people like: Noah, Moses, Abraham, David and Jesus. However, Islam does not accept the Bible's version of their lives and teachings – only the version given in the Koran. Muslims also receive a lot of direction from the sayings of Mohammed (Hadith) and the biographies of Mohammed. The thing I want to point out is that virtually all of Islam came to the world through a single man, at a single point in history. Of course, Muslims believe Mohammed received it all from God, but no one disputes that Islam came through Mohammed, and only through him.

Although Mormons often claim to be Christians, in that religion, the Book of Mormon is given more authority than the Bible. The Book of Mormon, according to Mormons, was discovered by Joseph Smith, with help from the angel Moroni. Mormonism does use Christianity as a jumping off point, but contains many things which contradict the Christian/Jewish Bible. The final authority of Mormonism comes from a book written by one man, at one place and time in history. Again,

Mormons claim that the book of Mormon is a divine revelation. Even so, only one man had that revelation.

No Muslim denies that the Koran – and Islam – originated through just one man at one particular time in history. As mentioned, Muslims believe that Mohammed was inspired by God. Unlike the Bible, however, the Koran was written in only one language, in one place, and arose from one culture. The Book of Mormon is similar: by the admission of Mormons it was revealed to just one man in one time and in one place.

Now, you might ask, what difference does it make how many people were involved in the formation of a religion, or authoritative religious book? Who cares whether one person wrote the Bible, or dozens did? Why does it matter if the Bible was written over the course of 1500 years, or just in one lifetime? What is the significance of what we've just learned?

From a simple, objective standpoint, if I am looking for guidance about how I can be the best person possible, it makes more sense to take the collected wisdom of many centuries, many life-situations, and many cultures, rather than the advice of just one person, one culture and one time in history.

Alexander McCall Smith is the author of many delightful fiction novels set in Africa. In one of his novels, the main character has these reflections on morality (from *Morality for Beautiful Girls* page 77-78)

> Most morality, thought Mma Ramotswe, was about doing the right thing because it had been identified as such by a long process of acceptance and observance. You simply could not create your own morality because your experience would never be

enough to do so. What gives you the right to say that you know better than your ancestors? Morality is for everybody, and this means that the views of more than one person are needed to create it. That was what made the modern morality, with its emphasis on individuals, and the working out of an individual position, so weak.

If you gave people the chance to work out their morality, then they would work out the version which was easiest for them and which allowed them to do what suited them for as much of the time as possible. That, in Mma Ramotswe's view was simple selfishness, whatever grand name one gave to it.

Mr. Smith gives us a tremendous and profound insight here. **Legitimate moral authority cannot come from one person.** No single human being, by himself or herself, has the breadth of experience, nor the wisdom, nor the character, to create morality.

Yet in Islam, all moral and spiritual authority comes from one man. Likewise with Mormonism. The same thing is also true of atheists, agnostics and secular humanists. If you are agnostic or atheistic, in a very real way you are saying that **you** are the source of moral authority. Your only guide, really, is what you decide. Your morality comes from one person: you.

But the Bible draws morality (guidance for human behavior) from dozens of people, dozens of centuries and many different cultures, languages and walks of life. It contains far more wisdom and experience than any one person could accumulate, even in a very long life.

When we reject the Bible as a guide to human behavior, we are saying that we know better than everybody else. We, in our few years of life upon this earth, are claiming to have wisdom, experience and authority greater than the collective wisdom and experience of entire cultures of people whose lives spanned more than a millennium and a half, whose morality and wisdom still profoundly shape the world we live in.

When I was in high school, the teachers said to us students that we needed to decide for ourselves what is right or wrong. We were told to create our own morality. The very thought of such a thing is nothing less than overwhelming, towering, ugly, arrogant pride. "Hubris" is another word for it. What, in all the universe, makes us think that we, in 16 years, could match the wisdom and experience that spanned 16 centuries and survived thousands of years more? What makes us think even a 90 year old person could match all that? Only ugly pride.

Remember, just for now, we are trying to evaluate this from a secular position, rather than a spiritual one. Does it seem rational to suppose that one person, in one lifetime, however varied her experience, however deep her wisdom, could match the wisdom and morality and experience contained in the Bible? Of course not. It's simple logic. And in this same respect, the Bible is logically superior to those other "holy books" which were brought into the world by single individuals.

Now some folks may say, "Well, I look at what's in the Bible, and make use of all that experience, but I still decide what is right for me." On the one hand, of course everybody does have to decide whether or not they will accept what is written in the Bible. But nonetheless, it seems awfully arrogant to say, "I know what the Bible says, but I still think I am wiser than Moses, Isaiah, Paul, Samuel, David, Peter, John, and Jesus (plus about two dozen more) all put together."

You see, even from a secular standpoint, the Bible is unique in history. There is no other ancient document so well preserved, so thoroughly verified as genuine by legitimate scholarly work (more on that in the coming chapters). There is no other source of moral and spiritual authority that has so much objective evidence that its teachings are based on such a breadth and depth of human experience.

> For my thoughts are not your thoughts, neither are your ways my ways, declares the Lord. As the heavens are higher than the earth, so my ways are higher than your ways, and my thoughts than your thoughts. (Isaiah 55:8-9)

This book, this Bible, goes far beyond the thoughts or ways of any one human being.

THE POINT:

Even considered from the perspective of someone with no Christian faith, the Bible is unique among religious books. In contrast to other religious writings, the Bible comes from a wide variety of people, places and times. This gives it a unique value when it comes to moral guidance, even apart from the question of whether or not it was inspired by God.

We will consider the question of God's inspiration in chapters 5 and 6.

3

Origins of the Old Testament

In the last chapter, we considered the Bible from a non-spiritual standpoint, evaluating it as if it were merely a system that was developed to guide human behavior (that is, a "moral" system). We found that objectively, the Bible offers a superior guide to human behavior than other "holy books" and one that is much superior to any "individual morality" that people choose for themselves.

In the next few chapters, I want to dig more deeply into the origins of the Bible. There is a lot of misinformation floating around about this subject. Some of the false information about the origins of scripture is put out in the form of television "documentaries" about "the lost books of the Bible," or "the suppressed truth about the Bible," or "the

Judas gospels." There is a grain of truth to many of these stories – though not much more than a grain. By looking at the real origins of the Bible, you will be able to evaluate these sorts of claims.

In this chapter, we will consider the Old Testament. We will tackle the New Testament in the next chapter. Once again, for the time being, I am going to stick mostly with objective, historical facts. We will look at issues of faith and spirituality in later chapters of this book.

Several early portions of the Old Testament were originally recited orally and passed down from generation to generation through memorization and repetition. Most of Genesis, as well as probably Ruth and Judges were all originally spoken, rather than written. How do we know this? Well, the first portions of Genesis, if accurate at all, took place before reading and writing was widespread. But even more than that, examining the Bible texts in Hebrew (which was the first language in which it was written down) shows several easily recognized mnemonic devices (that is, verbal cues used to help people memorize a recitation). One way to picture it is this: those texts which were originally recited orally, look (at least in Hebrew) more like a speech than an essay. Usually, the little memory devices are lost in translation to English, but one passage in which several English translations have preserved them fairly well is Genesis 5:1-31. There are seven small sections in these verses.

I will quote two of them from the Holman Christian Standard Bible (HCSB):

6Seth was 105 years old when he fathered
Enosh.7Seth lived 807 years after the birth of
Enosh, and he fathered other sons and
daughters.8So Seth's life lasted 912 years; then he
died.
9Enosh was 90 years old when he fathered
Kenan.10Enosh lived 815 years after the birth of
Kenan, and he fathered other sons and
daughters.11So Enosh's life lasted 905 years; then
he died. (Gen 5:6-11, HCSB)

Each section goes like this: "[*First Name*] was [*a number*]
years old when he fathered [*Second Name*]. [*First Name*] lived
[*a number*] of years after the birth of [*Second Name*] and he
fathered other sons and daughters. So [*First Name*]'s life
lasted [*a number*] years; then he died."

It is a kind of formula, clearly used to help people
remember the content. You memorize the formula, and then
all you have to do is plug in the correct names and number of
years.

If this is the first time you have heard of this, it may make
you a bit uncertain about how reliable those portions of
scripture could be. That is because our culture has mostly lost
the art and practice of memorization. But the fact is, there
used to be *professional* oral historians. These were people who
were responsible to memorize the oral histories, *word for
word* and teach them to the next generation. Not only that,
but in the case of the Hebrew people and the Old Testament,
every father had a duty to teach the spiritual history of their
people to his children. People are capable of remembering a
great deal. The philosopher Socrates, who lived almost a

thousand years after the time of Moses, lamented the fact that during his lifetime the Greeks started writing things down in books. He felt that if books came into widespread use, people would stop remembering things, because they would be able to simply look them up in a book. He felt that memorization was a much superior way to preserve knowledge for future generations.

The truth is, even in modern times we remember more, and better, than we realize. If you have seen the movie "Monty Python and the Holy Grail" I bet you can fill in this blank. Patsy, the trusty squire, is shot by an arrow. He says: "I'm not quite _____ yet." If you have seen the movie "The Princess Bride" I bet you know the word that the Sicilian kidnapper, Vicini, says all the time, or the special phrase Wesley uses to convey his love to Buttercup.

How many song lyrics have you memorized? You may be surprised when you start to think about it. All these are things we memorize – word for word – without even trying. In a culture where oral history is valued and practiced, the capacity for memorization is very great. The fact that the early portions of the Bible were originally in the form of oral history should not cause any concern about how accurately they were transmitted from one generation to the next.

Aside from the oral histories, other parts of the Old Testament were written down, more or less at the time the events occurred or the words were spoken. Some of the content comes from historical records kept by ancient Israeli government officials (like court historians). Other parts of the Old Testament are the teachings of prophets or the proclamations of kings, which were written down by scribes at the time they heard them. One of the largest books – the book of Psalms – is a compilation of worship songs and liturgies used in ancient Israel.

The first five books of the Old Testament are called "the Pentateuch;" they are also known by Jews as the "Torah," or "Law." Over time the Torah, and the writings of the scribes, historians, and prophets, were compiled into what today we call the Old Testament. Jewish people simply call this "the Bible," or, sometimes, "The Law and the Prophets."

We don't know the exact date at which the Old Testament was considered to be "closed," but it was certainly no later than 250 B.C., which is the approximate date most scholars agree that the Old Testament was first translated from Hebrew into Greek. (The ancient Greek version of the Old Testament is called "the Septuagint"). We don't have any *original* copies of the Old Testament. Professional scribes carefully copied the originals when they became worn, and then destroyed them. When the copies became worn (but long before they were difficult to read), new copies were made and the older copies destroyed. One of the reasons for doing this was to make sure every copy was perfectly clear, and there were not smudged or worn words to cast doubt upon what it said.

As a result of this process, for many years, the oldest Hebrew copy that had been found was made in the 800s A.D. – much newer, in fact, than many New Testament manuscripts. Because of this, many scholars assumed that if they could compare the Old Testament manuscript *copies* to the *originals*, there would be many errors. However, it should be noted that later manuscripts agree very closely with these earliest texts, which shows that the scribes took great care when making copies. In addition, the older Greek copies (the Septuagint) agree very closely with the newer Hebrew copies, although since the languages are different, word-for-word comparison is impossible.

In 1947, the "Dead Sea Scrolls" were discovered. These are not all Biblical writings, but among them are copies of parts of the Old Testament that, for some reason, were never destroyed as was the usual custom. The Dead Sea Scrolls date back to 1000 years before the oldest Hebrew Old Testament manuscripts that were then in existence. As it turns out, at least in the texts that are available for comparison, during those thousand years, very few copying errors had been made, and none were significant. Again it is an example of how carefully the Old Testament was preserved by the scribes. I have personally seen a scroll of Isaiah that was made in about 1400 A.D. and used in a synagogue in Germany for 400 years. In the mid-1800s, it was taken out of use because it was "worn." It looked cleaner, clearer and more pristine than this book. In other words, new copies were made long before manuscripts became difficult to read. Taken all in all, with help from the Septuagint and the Dead Sea Scrolls, it has been demonstrated convincingly that the contents of the Old Testament have been preserved, essentially unchanged, from when they originated.

Now, in spite of these well-preserved texts, there is a prevalent and long-standing tendency to discount the Old

Testament as "religious writing" and therefore inaccurate. For many decades the trendy thing was to doubt everything the Bible said – even the normal/historical parts of it – unless it could be confirmed by some sort of archaeological discovery. For instance, until very recently, skeptical scholars claimed that king David of Israel was a mythical figure who had been made up by the writers of the Bible. Unfortunately for them, archaeologists discovered a reference to David in the writings of another culture in the Middle East. The reference to David matched the approximate time period that the Bible puts him in. Since that time, architecture with inscriptions referring to David has also been found.

In the Old Testament, Isaiah writes about the invasion of the Assyrian army. He describes how they laid siege to the town of Lachish, and then how they came and surrounded Jerusalem. He mentions Sennacherib, the Assyrian emperor at the time. Over where Assyria used to be, they have uncovered some of the records and court-commissioned art from the same time. The Assyrians also kept a record of their emperor, Sennacherib. They also recorded some of the same events as Isaiah (like the siege of Lachish), and even mentioned the name of Hezekiah, who, according to both the Assyrians and the Bible, was King of Judah at the time.

According to the Old Testament, the Israelites destroyed the town of Jericho in about 1400 BC. According to archaeologists, Jericho was indeed destroyed about 1400 BC. There is not enough time and space to describe all of the archaeological discoveries which have, over and over, proven that the Bible is a reliable historical source. The people it talks about were real people; the situations it describes were real. The history it records really happened. The texts were truly written or memorized when the events they record were actually happening.

Millar Burrows, a Ph.D. graduate of Yale University, and one of the leading authorities on the Dead Sea Scrolls, said this:

> The Bible is supported by archaeological evidence again and again. On the whole, there can be no question that the results of excavation have increased the respect of scholars for the Bible as a collection of historical documents. The confirmation is both general and specific. The fact that the record can be so often explained or illustrated by archaeological data shows that it fits into the framework of history as only a genuine product of ancient life could do. In addition to this general authentication, however, we find the record verified repeatedly at specific points. Names of places and persons turn up at the right places and in the right periods.

What is strange is that some people persist in doubting the Bible until it is proven by some non-Biblical source. The truth is, there is no non-biblical source that has been so thoroughly verified as the Bible itself. It is, without question, the best documentary record of life and history in the ancient Middle East.

THE POINT:

There is a great deal of evidence to show that the Old Testament has been correctly and precisely preserved throughout the centuries. We also have plentiful support for the historical accuracy of the Old Testament.

4

Origins of the New Testament

We have learned a little about the Old Testament. But where did the New Testament come from?

The short answer is this: Jesus chose twelve people who knew him personally to be his apostles. He lived with them, taught them and trained them. One of them (Judas) betrayed Jesus and then committed suicide. Along with the apostles, there were a number of other people who spent significant time with Jesus, but who were not part of the chosen twelve. We might call them his *close disciples*. After Jesus was no longer on this earth, his apostles, and a few of his close disciples, taught and wrote about him. They wrote down their teaching in letters and "gospels" (accounts of the life and teachings of Jesus). These writings about Jesus and his teachings became what we call the New Testament.

A few people came to be considered apostles after Jesus' crucifixion. One of them, Paul, did not even know Jesus before his crucifixion – he became a follower of Jesus later on. Paul wrote a large portion of the New Testament, in the form of letters to various churches and individuals. Because of this, and because he did not know Jesus before the crucifixion, it may be worthwhile to take a closer look at Paul's credentials.

Luke records that Saul, an enemy of Christians, had an encounter with Jesus on the way to persecute and imprison Christians in Damascus (Acts, chapter nine). After the encounter, Saul became a Christian, and went by his Roman name, Paul. In Galatians 1:11-24, Paul claims that shortly after his encounter on the Damascus road, Jesus came to him in a special way and revealed the gospel to him.

We might, at first, be skeptical of Paul's claims. However, Barnabas fully affirmed Paul and his theology. Barnabas was not one of the original twelve apostles, but there is evidence that he knew Jesus before the crucifixion, and he may have been one of Jesus' close disciples. Barnabas was certainly considered a leader in the early Christian church in both Jerusalem and Antioch, and Luke calls him an apostle, in the book of Acts. In addition, the nephew of Barnabas was John-Mark, who wrote the gospel of Mark. He traveled with Paul on one of his missionary journeys.

There was a temporary falling out between Barnabas and Paul over the unreliability of John-Mark, however, the dispute was not about theology, but about whether or not it was advisable to take Mark on a second journey.

The Jerusalem council of Acts chapter 15, made up of the apostles whom Jesus had chosen personally (as well as a few others), endorsed Paul, Barnabas and their teachings.

Luke, who wrote the gospel of Luke, and the book of Acts, also traveled extensively with Paul, and there is no indication that he had a problem with Paul's teachings. Peter, in his second letter, affirms the teachings of Paul (2 Peter 3:15-16).

To sum up Paul's qualifications: He received a special revelation from Jesus. He is closely associated with two of the four gospel writers (Mark and Luke), and they did not dispute Paul's teachings, and in fact, affirmed his theology. He is closely associated with a very prominent early church leader (Barnabas), who also affirmed Paul's teaching. Paul's teaching was officially endorsed by the apostle Peter, and also by the entire apostolic leadership at the Jerusalem council of 49 AD.

Paul's first letter (Galatians) was probably written after that Jerusalem council, most likely the same year. Every other New Testament document written by Paul was indisputably written after the Jerusalem council had endorsed his qualifications.

Besides Paul, there are four authors in the New Testament who were not in the group of original apostles. Mark (who wrote the gospel of Mark) was not in that group. We have already mentioned him, briefly. Mark was the nephew of Barnabas, and both of them were probably part of the larger group of close disciples that often traveled with Jesus. Many scholars think he was the young man who ran away naked when the soldiers came to arrest Jesus (Mark 15:51-52). In addition, Mark traveled with Paul and Barnabas, and spent extensive time with the apostle Peter. His gospel is believed to be a basic summary of the things he himself heard, and also what he heard Peter say about Jesus.

The man who wrote the book of James was not James the apostle. The apostle James was beheaded within about ten years of Jesus' death. But the James who wrote the book was the son of Mary, mother of Jesus. In other words, he was Jesus' half-brother (Galatians 1:19). Obviously, he knew Jesus, and James experienced a special encounter with Jesus after the resurrection (1 Corinthians 15:7). James' brother Jude (thus, another one of Jesus' half-brothers) also wrote a short letter that is part of the New Testament.

Luke was the only other person who was not an apostle who contributed to the New Testament. He wrote the gospel of Luke, and the book of Acts. It is clear from both that he spent extensive time with Barnabas, Mark, the apostle Paul, and with many other Christians, including Mary, mother of Jesus, and other close disciples.

No one knows for sure who wrote the letter to the Hebrews. Many people believe it was Paul, though it is missing Paul's usual personal greetings. Others think it might have been James, Barnabas, or another of the apostles. We do know however, that it has been accepted as a genuine apostolic letter for as long as the other books in the New Testament.

That brings us to the next point. How do we know that the teachings of these people who knew Jesus are, in fact, accurately preserved?

Skeptics generally criticize the New Testament with these ideas: [They say] it was created a long time after Jesus, by people who never knew him. If there was any truth to it, it has been distorted by people who changed the stories to suit their own purposes. Usually, they say the reason it was created was to give power and control to religious leaders.

The actual facts obliterate these ideas. In the first place, the idea that the New Testament was created to give control to religious people, is nonsensical. We can trace many New Testament books (in their present form) back to around 150 AD. We can trace certain passages to before 99 AD. It is well established that the entire New Testament as we know it was used from 250 AD onwards. The problem for skeptics is that up until 320 AD, Christianity itself was illegal in the Roman Empire (which is where it began). During all this time in history, people were often deprived of freedom and property for being Christians. Christian leaders were sometimes tortured and martyred. Far from giving them power, the New Testament gave them the status of outcasts. If the original purpose for the New Testament was power for religious leaders, it would contain verses that affirm Emperor-worship and pagan gods. Instead, during the time it was supposedly "made up," it led to the opposite of power and control. There is overwhelming evidence to show that it was not changed after Christianity became legal (more on that, next).

Secondly, we can know for sure that the stories and teachings of Jesus, and the teachings about him, were not changed and distorted with the passing of time. We can know this through comparing the surviving copies.

Ancient documents were written by hand. Because writing materials wear out, when those documents started to degrade, new copies were made. Because of this, over the years, many, many copies of the New Testament were produced. In addition, because Christianity is a faith that is supposed to spread, numerous copies were made to be carried all over the known world. Not only that, but the New Testament was also translated into several languages, and copies were made, and recopied in those other languages, also. Unlike the Jews with the Old Testament, Christians did not destroy copies of the New Testament.

If you can find numerous copies of an ancient document, you can compare them to each other, to see if they are the same. It helps if they come from different places and different time periods.

Much of what we know of the history of 0-100 A.D. comes from just a few ancient documents. One of them is called *Annals*. A Roman named Tacitus wrote it in about A.D. 100. Tacitus is considered to be a very good historical source for that period. Today, **twenty** ancient texts of Tacitus' writing exist. The *oldest* is a copy that was made in 1100 A.D. – **1000 years after Tacitus wrote the original**. With regard to *Annals*, no historian seriously disputes that they were indeed written by Tacitus. Scholars have compared the twenty surviving ancient manuscripts, and most accept that what Tacitus originally wrote has been accurately preserved.

There is no document that old (besides the New Testament) that has even 300 ancient copies still in existence. There is no document that old (besides the New Testament) in which the copies date within 500 years of the original.

Compare this to the New Testament, which contains books originally written between 50 and 90 A.D. There are more than five thousand six hundred (5,686, to be exact) ancient copies of these documents in the original language (which was Greek). The *oldest* copy of any part of the New Testament is a fragment of the book of John (known as the Ryland's Manuscript) which is dated very close to the time which John actually wrote the book – certainly within forty years, but possibly even part of the original. Another fragment of Matthew is believed to be so close in time as to be part of the original gospel as written down by Matthew himself. Many of the books exist in copies that were made within 100 years of the original. There are complete New Testament manuscripts – i.e. all the books gathered together as part of one document – that date less than 200 years after the time of the apostles. In addition to all this, we have ancient translations of the New Testament in Latin, Coptic (an ancient Egyptian language), Arabic, Slavic, Armenian and several more ancient languages. In fact there are 19,284 ancient copies of all or part of the New Testament in ancient languages other than Greek. The oldest are in Latin and

Syriac, and are dated around 150 AD – or, **less than 100 years after the originals were written in Greek**.

To put it another way, there are 284 times more copies of the Greek New Testament than there are of Tacitus. And the age of the copies is almost a thousand times better. That makes the New Testament a much better historical document than the best other documents from that same period.

The fact that there are so many ancient copies also makes it possible to know with a good deal of certainty what the original documents said. In other words, with so many good copies out there, we can compare the texts and see if they are the same or not. If all or most of the texts show that John wrote "Jesus wept," than we can be very sure that John did, in fact, write "Jesus wept."

If we have a manuscript dating from 200 AD that says, "Jesus said I am the light of the world," and another manuscript from 500 AD that says the same thing, we can tell that the text was not changed during that period of time, even though the earlier manuscript was made before Christianity was legal in the Roman Empire.

Scholars have now been comparing and compiling these ancient manuscripts for some time, and we can be very confident that what we read in English has been translated from a Greek text that is about 98% exactly the same as what was originally written in the first century A.D. There are some differences between ancient copies, of course. Some of them are easily identified as copying errors. Some of the differences show up in only a few of the manuscripts, while all of the others agree. In such cases, the errors are easily identified and dismissed. But there are a few differences in the ancient copies of the New Testament that can't be easily resolved. None of those textual differences have any impact on any major Christian beliefs. None of them change doctrine. Many English Bible translations make note of any major differences between ancient Greek manuscripts.

For instance, let's consider Luke 23:38. Luke records that when Jesus was put on the cross, a notice was posted above him. From the Holman Christian Standard Bible (HCSB):

> An inscription was written above Him: 'This is the king of the Jews.'

There is a footnote mark in the HCSB, right after "Him." The footnote reads:

> **23:38** Other mss add written in Greek, Latin, and Hebrew letters

This tells us that some ancient manuscripts contain those additional words, but in the opinion of the translators, they probably weren't part of the original text. This is what we call a "major variant."

You may say: "What's the big deal with that? What's so *major* about it? What does it change? Let's think about it. The text used by the HCSB doesn't say anything specific about the language of the notice. So even if the variant reading is correct, it does not contradict anything. Even if there were a necessary contradiction between the best reading and the variant reading, it still doesn't change any important Christian belief. It doesn't really matter in which language (or languages) the notice was written.

The truth is, virtually all of the "major variants" are in fact, extremely *minor* when it comes to meaning and significance.

One of the biggest major variants comes from John 7:53-8:11 (the story of the woman caught in adultery). The New International Version (NIV) makes this note: "The earliest and most reliable manuscripts and other ancient witnesses do not have John 7:53-8:11." In all probability this little section was not included by John when he wrote the gospel. It may have been a story told by John that was well known to those who knew him. After his death, they might have included it in the gospel so that the story would not be lost. It might have been written by John at some other time, or by one of the other apostles and included in John's gospel so the story wouldn't get lost. **But even if you take this little section out of the Bible, it doesn't change any major doctrine**.

Another pretty big variant comes at the end of Mark, in Mark 16:9-20. Again, almost any English Bible translation will somehow indicate that these verses may not have been part of the original gospel written by Mark. The HCSB puts it within brackets:

> 9[Early on the first day of the week, after He had risen, He appeared first to Mary Magdalene, out of whom He had driven seven demons. 10She went and reported to those who had been with Him, as they were mourning and weeping. 11Yet, when they heard that He was alive and had been seen by her, they did not believe it. 12Then after this, He appeared in a different form to two of them walking on their way into the country. 13And they went and

reported it to the rest, who did not believe them either.

14Later, He appeared to the Eleven themselves as they were reclining at the table. He rebuked their unbelief and hardness of heart, because they did not believe those who saw Him after He had been resurrected.

15Then He said to them, "Go into all the world and preach the gospel to the whole creation. 16Whoever believes and is baptized will be saved, but whoever does not believe will be condemned. 17And these signs will accompany those who believe: In My name they will drive out demons; they will speak in new languages; 18they will pick up snakes; if they should drink anything deadly, it will never harm them; they will lay hands on the sick, and they will get well."

19Then after speaking to them, the Lord Jesus was taken up into heaven and sat down at the right hand of God. 20And they went out and preached everywhere, the Lord working with them and confirming the word by the accompanying signs.]
(Mark 16:8-20, HCSB)

Verses 9-13 record that the disciples did not at first believe Mary, but that later, Jesus appeared to some of them, and they eventually believed in his resurrection. This matches what is written in Matthew, Luke and John, so even if we take these verses out of Mark, we haven't lost anything. Verses 14-16 also match things that are written in other places within the New Testament.

In fact the only things in this passage that are not taught elsewhere in the New Testament are found in verse 18 – the part about handling snakes and drinking poison. If we leave out those words, it changes no significant Christian doctrine.

In fact, if we left this *entire section* out of the end of the gospel of Mark, it changes no major Christian belief.

There are a few other major variants, but they are all similarly insignificant. If you would like more information about variants, and how the text of the Bible is determined, please see "Appendix A: Extra Information about the Basis for Modern Translations."

In addition to all the copies of the New Testament, we have the many surviving letters and documents of early Christian leaders. These early Christians quoted both the Old and New Testaments extensively in their writings. It is obvious from this that the books of the New Testament must have existed during the lifetimes of the people who quoted them. Since we know when these early church leaders lived, we know that the New Testament is at least as old as they are. The oldest of these is Clement of Rome, who died in 99 A.D. Thus, we know that the eight books of the New Testament that Clement quoted had to exist before the year 99. Another early church leader was Ignatius of Antioch, who died, at latest, in 116 A.D. The thirteen books of the New Testament that *he* quoted, obviously existed before the year 116. The gospel of John is widely accepted by scholars to be the last book of the New Testament to be written. Ignatius quotes John's gospel, which strongly suggests that by A.D. 116, all of the books of the New Testament were established and in use among Christians throughout the Roman Empire.

There are other ancient writings about Jesus – writings that were **not** included in the New Testament. These include *The Shepherd of Hermas*, *Didache, Apocalypse of Peter, The*

Gospel of Judas, The Gnostic Gospel of Thomas and several more.

From time to time, the National Geographic Society will do an article or documentary featuring some of these writings. You can find other television programs about them, and numerous articles on the internet. Unfortunately, most of these programs and articles seem to have been created for the purpose of casting doubt on the New Testament. Although the study of these ancient books may be interesting, it must be said that often they are presented by media in ways that range from deceptive to downright false.

What the shows and articles will often not explain, is that these texts do not boast the same number of ancient copies as the New Testament books, nor are they as well preserved or as close to the time of the originals. These writings generally have little historical validation in their connections with Jesus, the apostles or Christianity; certainly none of the type enjoyed by the New Testament writings. Many of them were found only in local areas, not across the entire ancient Roman world, like the books of the New Testament.

There were several things that caused a book to be included in the New Testament.

1. The New Testament book had to be connected to an apostle, or someone closely connected to Jesus (we looked at this earlier). *The Apocalypse of Peter*, though it names an apostle in the title, was never recognized in any early writing or by any evidence as having anything to do with the real historical Peter.

It was rejected because the people at the time knew that Peter had no connection to it.

2. The New Testament book had to enjoy widespread use among churches. (For example, the Gospel of John was used and recognized in churches all over the known world by a very early date; whereas the "Gospel of Judas" was never really recognized outside of Alexandria, Egypt and that at a fairly late date, by people who weren't even Christians.)

3. The New Testament writings had to agree with generally accepted Christian doctrine. In the 140s A.D. a man named Marcion came up with his own very twisted version of Christianity, and listed various writings which he thought should be considered sacred. He and his "New Testament" were rejected because they were contrary to the teachings that the churches had held since the time of the apostles.

So, we have an overwhelming amount of evidence that the texts of the New Testament we read today are almost exactly the same as when they were first written in the decades following the crucifixion of Jesus. There is really no question about the provenance of the New Testament.

So we know that what we have is what was originally written. But is it historically accurate? Well, no ancient document has been as verifiably well preserved as the New Testament. Since we get a lot of our knowledge about history from ancient documents, that, in and of itself, should give us confidence that the New Testament is historically reliable. If the writings of Tacitus, or Julius Caesar are to be accepted as reliable sources of ancient history, then the New Testament should be accepted in the same way; even more so.

However, many skeptical people, including scholars, insist upon a position of assuming that the New Testament is wrong until proved right. No doubt, this is because they do not want to believe what it says about Jesus or the supernatural. Even so, time and time again, the New Testament has been proven right, while the skeptics have been proved wrong. Let me give you a few instances.

Luke Chapter 2 talks about a census taken by Caesar Augustus. He said that it happened while Quirinius was governor of Syria. This is a concrete historical event which Luke connects to a real person: Quirinius. The first century Roman records (not as well preserved as the New Testament) do indicate a census during the time of Emperor Augustus. Thus far, we see that Luke is talking about actual things that happened at a real point in history.

But there has been no Roman record uncovered that mentions a governor of Syria named Quirinius. Skeptics long held that this proved that the New Testament is unreliable. The general idea was that Luke was written by someone who lived long after he claimed to, and he made up the name of a governor of Syria to add "color" to the story of his gospel.

Let's consider the logic of that claim. Those skeptics did not have actual evidence that contradicted the New Testament. What they had was a *lack* of evidence to *confirm* it. Lack of evidence does not prove anything. Since the skeptics also had a lack of evidence to support their own position, they were standing on shaky logical ground.

Eventually, some coins were excavated in the ancient Roman province of Syria. In the first century, provincial coins were stamped with the name and likeness of the governor who ruled at the time the coin was made. The coins discovered in Syria were from the reign of Caesar Augustus, right at the beginning of the "common era" and they were stamped with the name "Quirinius." In other words, we now have positive proof that Luke wrote accurately. The skeptics were wrong.

Another place where skeptics held there was a "lack of evidence" was for the existence of a high priest named Caiaphas. Caiaphas was involved in the trial of Jesus. Archaeologists had not found any record of him outside the New Testament. Again, the skeptics had no evidence against the New Testament, just a lack of confirmation. Then, in the early 1990s, excavations were made to build a water park in Jerusalem. The excavators discovered an ossuary – a "bone box." It was labeled as holding the bones of Caiaphas, who was identified as a high priest in Jerusalem.

There are many more areas where skeptics never even had a chance. The New Testament names dozens of Roman officials, and makes references to hundreds of little cultural details that have all been affirmed by archaeology and other ancient documents. There can be no question that the New Testament is entirely historically reliable.

THE POINT:

There is an overwhelming amount of evidence in support of the fact that the text of the New Testament books, as we have them today, are virtually exact copies of the texts as they were originally written by those who personally knew Jesus Christ.

There is an abundance of evidence which contradicts the idea that the books and stories of the New Testament were changed or distorted in order to grant power to religious leaders.

In addition, in both general and specific matters, the New Testament has been shown to be historically reliable and accurate.

5

What about the Supernatural?

We've learned where the Old and New Testaments came from. We know by objective, scientific criteria that the documents we have today are accurately preserved copies of what was first written or spoken. We understand from archaeology that both the Old and New Testaments are historically reliable. **These things are facts, not religious opinion**. Most of these facts were discovered by people who were trying to prove the opposite.

But of course, the Bible is not merely a history book. It claims to be a message from God. In addition to history, the Bible tells us other things that we cannot verify with science; things about God, human nature, human relationships and human-God interactions. It even talks about things that we rarely see (if at all) in our lifetimes, namely, miracles. Among the many miracles the Bible records are things like the parting of the Red Sea, the feeding of the five thousand, healings and exorcisms. I think this is one of the main reasons people ignore the Bible. These aren't everyday events. It's hard to believe that stuff like that ever happened. Maybe you have struggled with the same thing. We will consider this problem in this chapter.

Consider a person whom you think is entirely reliable. If she tells you that chicken is only $0.99/pound at Kroger on Wednesday, you know that you can go to Kroger and find chicken for exactly that price. If she tells you that she once met the mayor of New York City, it does not surprise you at all when she produces a picture of herself with the Mayor, and a signed note from him to her. If you ask her to give you the square root of 361, you can bet your next paycheck that she'll say 19.

Now, suppose, one day, your friend tells you that she just found out she has cancer. You know she wouldn't lie to you. You know she wouldn't be mistaken. You absolutely believe she has cancer. A few weeks later, she tells you that she went to a prayer meeting, and people prayed for her healing. A few days after that, she went to the doctor, and found out she is now entirely cancer-free. She claims she has been miraculously healed. Would you believe her?

You would believe your friend about the price of chicken, the mayor of New York and the square root of 361. You would believe her when she told you she had cancer. So why wouldn't you believe her when she says she was miraculously healed?

I think there is one main reason you might be reluctant to believe your reliable friend about the miracle. You think perhaps that though she can be objective about chicken and mathematics, she might not be able to be as objective about her own belief that she was healed. **However, let's be very clear: this attitude reveals *your* underlying belief that miracles don't happen**. Your world view accepts the times-table, and the fact that chicken has a price, so you don't question your friend who has proved reliable on those things. But since you don't believe in miracles, you think your friend cannot be objective about them. **Understand this: it is *your* belief, not hers, that influences how you judge her story about her healing**. You are not starting with evidence (which is the testimony of a reliable witness about a miracle), instead, you are starting with your belief ("there are no miracles") and trying to make the evidence fit your world view, by assuming she is honestly mistaken.

It is popularly believed that people who accept miracles do so because they have a belief in them, while people who reject them do so because of good, objective evidence against them. However, that is the reverse of the truth. There are thousands upon thousands of testimonies given by reliable people about miracles, in every period of history. This is the evidence. Their testimony is rejected out of hand by people who have simply said: "I refuse to believe such things." **There *is* blind faith involved, but it is on the part of those who *dis*believe in miracles**.

Let's apply this to how we look at the Bible. The Bible has proven many times to be entirely reliable about things like the culture of the ancient Middle East, the existence of specific cities and specific people. It has shown again and again to be a reliable record of battles, and kings and wars. We know it records the truth of those kinds of things. The only reason to doubt what it says about God, human nature, and miracles is because we have already decided that we do not want to believe those things. This is an irrational, illogical position to take.

Even so, I understand, it is a big leap to go from believing what the Bible says about a Roman official, to believing what it says about something supernatural, like miracles. It is what we call, "a leap of faith."

Let me give you some more help. There are other ancient religious texts besides the Bible that claim to have supernatural authority, and record various supernatural events. The Bible is different from those in two important ways. First, as we have seen, the Bible has a great deal of historical credibility, far more so than any other ancient religious text.

Second, the Bible, particularly the Old Testament, contains numerous predictive prophecies which have been fulfilled.

It cannot be disputed that the Old Testament was complete more than two hundred years before the time of Jesus Christ. The Old Testament predicted that he would be a descendant of King David, born in Bethlehem, spend time in Egypt, and yet be called a citizen of the town of Nazareth. It predicted the slaughter of innocent children that was perpetrated by King Herod. It predicted that the ministry of Jesus would be preceded by a desert preacher (who turned out to be John the Baptist), and that Jesus would begin his ministry in the northern region of Israel (Galilee). The whipping of Jesus, his rejection by his own people, and his suffering and death were all also predicted long before his birth. All of these things, and more, were fulfilled in the life of Jesus Christ.

There are many other prophecies made by the Bible which have already been fulfilled. I have given you only a few of those that relate to Jesus, because even the most hardened skeptic cannot dispute that the prophecies came before the fulfillments. A great many of them could not have been arranged in advance by Jesus (for instance, where he was born, where his parents took him as a child, his whipping and crucifixion, and many other things).

However, a skeptic might say: "Ah, but the writers of the New Testament probably made up facts about the life of Jesus to fit the prophecies." There are several important ways to answer this idea.

First, the gospels (which record the life of Jesus) simply do not read like made-up stories. As I have already pointed out in the previous chapters, they are grounded in real history – we *know for certain* that a great deal of it was **not** imaginary. If the real history is mixed with myth, it is the most masterful example of such literature in existence, since the parts that were supposedly imaginary read just like the parts we know are historical.

Second, and more importantly, **the apostles died for insisting upon the truth of these things**. We know that these writings come to us, unedited, from the time of the apostles (this was demonstrated in the last chapter). And we know that most of the apostles suffered persecution, hardship and death because of what they wrote and taught. **If they made up large portions of it, what in all the earth would have made them willing to die for what they knew to be a lie?**

It is simply not plausible to suggest that the apostles knowingly wrote lies about Jesus. We are left then, with the conclusion that the life and death of Jesus Christ happened just as they recorded it, and fulfilled a great number of prophecies that were made hundreds of years before Jesus.

If you want more examples of fulfilled prophecies, consider this one: The destruction of Jerusalem was predicted by the prophet Isaiah. During Isaiah's lifetime, the great threat to Jerusalem was the Assyrian empire, led by Sennacherib. At one point, Sennacherib and the Assyrians even laid siege to the city. But Isaiah predicted that it would be destroyed, not by the *Assyrians*, but by the *Babylonians*, who were not even a threat during his lifetime. Isaiah, along with several others, predicted that after Jerusalem was destroyed, many of the country's people would be exiled by the Babylonians, and that the exile would last for about seventy years, which is exactly what happened.

These predictive prophecies make the Bible different than the sacred writings of other religions. The Koran did not predict the birth of Mohammed – it was Mohammed who gave us the Koran. It does not predict specific military victories or defeats. It does not predict specific things about certain people. **Aside from the Bible, no religious book does**.

The fulfilled prophecies of the Bible make it unique, and strongly suggest that this is a book worth learning more about. All this is to say, give the Bible a chance when it speaks about supernatural things.

THE POINT:

The Bible isn't just a history book. It claims to speak of supernatural things. There is considerable evidence that some of the writers of the Bible made predictive prophesies which were later fulfilled. This should encourage us to keep an open mind when we read about supernatural occurrences in the Bible.

6

The Mystery

Once again, I want to remind you of the blind men and the elephant. If you stick with me, you'll get a clear picture of what the Bible is all about, and how to understand it, and sort through the confusion created by others.

I'd like to continue, therefore, by backing up and looking at the big picture. Let's start by examining what the Bible says about itself, and its purpose. That alone will clarify a number of things about the Bible. I will summarize, and then unpack each point:

- First, the Bible claims of itself that it was *inspired by God*. It says it is *God's Word* to humanity.

- Second, the purpose of the entire Bible, even the Old Testament, *is to help us get to know Jesus better.*
- Third, the Bible *provides us with instruction, training and teaching in how to be disciples of Jesus.* It gives encouragement and hope to Jesus-followers.

~

Let's start with the first point. The Bible says that it is God's message to us, given through people who were inspired by the Holy Spirit to write the words they wrote. Here are a few places that make this clear:

> 1Long ago God spoke to the fathers by the prophets at different times and in different ways. 2In these last days, He has spoken to us by His Son. God has appointed Him heir of all things and made the universe through Him. (Heb 1:1-2, HCSB)

> First of all, you should know this: No prophecy of Scripture comes from one's own interpretation, because no prophecy ever came by the will of man; instead, men spoke from God as they were moved by the Holy Spirit. (2Pet 1:20-21, HCSB)

> 16All Scripture is inspired by God and is profitable for teaching, for rebuking, for correcting, for training in righteousness, 17so that the man of God may be complete, equipped for every good work. (2Tim 3:16-17, HCSB)

Christians call the Bible "the Word of God," meaning that even though human beings wrote it, it was God who inspired them as they wrote. **That is what the Bible claims to be: the Word of God.**

~

Next, let's look at the *primary purpose* for the Bible, God's Word. **The purpose of the Bible is to reveal Jesus Christ and help us get to know him better**.

Now, at first, this may surprise you, because about two thirds of the Bible was written long before Jesus lived. Let me back up, and explain.

I'm a mystery novelist. If you haven't already, I'd love it if you can help me become ridiculously rich and famous by buying my other books and then telling everyone you know about them, and posting about them online. But that's not my point. My point is, when I write a novel, the mystery is not revealed until near the end. If you read two-thirds of one of my *Lake Superior Mysteries*, and then stopped, the story-line would not make sense. You can't fully understand the beginning until you have read the entire book.

On the other hand, if you read the *last* one-third of one of my books, but not the beginning, you would get the main gist of the story. You would understand the basic, underlying plot, and the mystery would be unveiled for you. However, you would miss out on many rich nuances and many enjoyable parts of the story. If you hadn't read the beginning, you might not understand why some of the events at the end were so significant for the characters. You'd get the idea, but you would still be missing out on a lot.

The Bible is not a novel and I don't recommend reading it from beginning to end. Even so, you cannot get the whole "story" of the Bible until you have read the end, that is, the New Testament. The Old Testament, written before Jesus walked on earth, is the record of how God prepared the world. He laid the foundations of culture and history and geopolitics until the world was uniquely primed to understand and spread the message of his grace, given in Jesus Christ. Then he sent Jesus. Jesus is the revelation of what God was doing. He is the unveiling of the mystery. The New Testament writers even refer to the message about Jesus as a "mystery":

> By reading this you are able to understand my insight about the mystery of the Messiah. This was not made known to people in other generations as it is now revealed to His holy apostles and prophets by the Spirit: (Eph 3:4-5, HCSB)

> Instead we speak the wisdom of God, hidden in a mystery, that God determined before the ages for our glory. None of the rulers of this age understood it. If they had known it, they would not have crucified the Lord of glory. (1Cor 2:7-8, NET)

For the writers of the Bible "mystery" did not mean a puzzle you must solve, but rather, something hidden until the proper time for it to be revealed. **This idea of "mystery" is one of the keys to understanding the whole Bible, and the relationship between the Old and New Testaments. The New Testament is the revelation of the mystery: namely, Jesus Christ**. It shows us what God was ultimately aiming at, in the Old Testament. We cannot understand the Old Testament without the New Testament, the revelation of Jesus Christ. You can get the basic message from the New Testament, even if you haven't read the Old. In fact, I think it is best to read the New Testament first. It won't "spoil the ending," in fact, it will help you to understand the whole Bible. But you won't fully understand the incredible grace and wisdom and power of God unless you read both the Old and the New Testaments.

Once again, the mystery, the key to the entire Bible, is Jesus himself. Jesus said to the Jews who believed the Old Testament:

> The Father who sent Me has Himself testified about Me. You have not heard His voice at any time, and you haven't seen His form. You don't have His word living in you, because you don't believe the One He sent. You pore over the Scriptures because you think you have eternal life in them, *yet they testify about Me.* (John 5:37-39, HCSB)

Jesus said that the Old Testament Scriptures *testify about him.* Both before and after his resurrection, Jesus pointed out to his disciples how the scriptures (that is, the Old Testament) looked ahead to the Messiah, to Himself:

> He said to them, "How unwise and slow you are to believe in your hearts all that the prophets have spoken! Didn't the Messiah have to suffer these things and enter into His glory? " Then beginning with Moses and all the Prophets, He interpreted for them *the things concerning Himself in all the Scriptures.* (Luke 24:25-27, HCSB)

> Then He told them, "These are My words that I spoke to you while I was still with you — that everything written about Me in the Law of Moses, the Prophets, and the Psalms must be fulfilled." Then He opened their minds to understand the Scriptures. (Luke 24:44-45, HCSB)

Paul also used the Old Testament to share the good news about Jesus:

> For he vigorously refuted the Jews in public, demonstrating through the Scriptures that Jesus is the Messiah. (Acts 18:28, HCSB)

The specifics of how Paul did that are all throughout his letters. That is one reason why it is helpful to read the New Testament first – it gives us a guide for understanding what came before. The key is Jesus. Therefore, one very helpful trick when reading the *Old* Testament is to ask these sorts of questions of every passage:

- Where is Jesus in this passage?
- How does it teach me something about Jesus?
- Does one of the people in this story act in a way that reminds me what Jesus is like?
- Is it a prophecy about his life on earth, or what he will do at the end of time?
- What does it tell me about my need for a savior like Jesus?

Let's make this practical by considering a passage from the book of Isaiah:

> Yet He Himself bore our sicknesses, and He carried our pains; but we in turn regarded Him stricken, struck down by God, and afflicted. But He was pierced because of our transgressions, crushed because of our iniquities; punishment for our peace was on Him, and we are healed by His wounds. We all went astray like sheep; we all have turned to our own way; and the LORD has punished Him for the iniquity of us all. He was oppressed and afflicted, yet He did not open His mouth. Like a lamb led to the slaughter and like a sheep silent before her

shearers, He did not open His mouth. (Isa 53:4-7, HCSB)

...My righteous servant will justify many, and he will carry their iniquities (Isa 53:11)

This was written hundreds of years before Jesus was born. There is not a reputable scholar in the world who disputes that. And yet, it is clearly the message that someone (Isaiah doesn't know whom) would take the sins of others upon himself, and through his suffering, bring us peace with God. That "someone" would not object to the suffering imposed upon him, but engage in it willingly.

This passage is in the Old Testament. So where is Jesus? Clearly, Jesus is the "someone" that Isaiah writes about. What does it tell us about him? It tells us that he suffered for our sake, that he died on our behalf, and that through Him we have forgiveness, healing and peace. We were the ones who went astray, but it was Jesus who suffered for it, so that we could be restored to God. Isaiah 53 is a great example of how something that was written long before the time of Jesus is still all about him, and what he would do for us. So we read the Bible, even the Old Testament, and find Jesus.

Jesus is the main point of the entire Bible. **Reading the Bible should help us get to know Jesus better.** It should encourage us in our faith in Jesus. Reading the Bible should strengthen us spiritually, from the inside out. That is what it is for. So read it with that in mind.

~

The second purpose of the Bible is to help us to follow Jesus in our everyday lives, as God desires. When we put our trust in Jesus, and let him lead our lives, it has enormous implications for everything else in life. So the main point of the Bible is Jesus. In addition, there are many "secondary" points that flesh out what trust in Jesus means for us, in hundreds of practical, emotional and spiritual ways. So Paul writes:

> But as for you, continue in what you have learned and firmly believed. You know those who taught you, and you know that from childhood you have known the sacred Scriptures, which are able to give you wisdom for salvation through faith in Christ Jesus. All Scripture is inspired by God and is profitable for teaching, for rebuking, for correcting, for training in righteousness, so that the man of God may be complete, equipped for every good work. (2Tim 3:14-17, HCSB)

Of course, Paul didn't know that his own letter to Timothy would be included in the Bible. He was talking about the Old Testament. But Christians today believe that the Holy Spirit inspired Paul to write this, and that it is intended for *both the Old and New Testaments*. Jesus spoke prophetically about this:

> "Therefore," He said to them, "every student of Scripture instructed in the kingdom of heaven is like a landowner who brings out of his storeroom what is new and what is old." (Matt 13:52, HCSB)

The "old treasure" in the storehouse are the writings of the Old Testament. The "New Treasure" is the mystery, now revealed, of Jesus Christ. I quoted from Peter's second letter earlier in the chapter, but here it is again:

> First of all, you should know this: No prophecy of Scripture comes from one's own interpretation, because no prophecy ever came by the will of man;

> instead, men spoke from God as they were moved
> by the Holy Spirit. (2Pet 1:20-21, HCSB)

Christians have believed for almost two-thousand years that this is true of the New Testament, as well as the Old.

So, first we read in order to get to know Jesus better. And if we are Jesus-followers, the whole Bible (both Old and New Testaments) is also useful for:

- Teaching
- Rebuking
- Correcting
- Training in righteousness
- Equipping the godly person to do good works.

Paul said it a different way in his letter to the Romans:

> For whatever was written in the past was written for
> our instruction, so that we may have hope through
> endurance and through the encouragement from
> the Scriptures. (Rom 15:4, HCSB)

So in addition to the things above, we also:

- Learn from the Bible
- Gain hope from it
- Learn endurance from it
- Become encouraged by it.

With that in mind, let's look at an example of *instruction*.

Deuteronomy 25:4 says "Do not muzzle an ox while it treads out grain." Now, not too many people who read my books own oxen. I bet none of you even own a muzzle for an ox. So what is the point of this verse for you today? Remember, it was written for your instruction. All scripture is given by God and is useful for teaching, training, correcting and encouraging. So we should not read a verse like this and say: "Well, I don't have an ox, so never mind about that one." Instead, we should read a verse like this and pray something like the following: "Holy Spirit, I'm not getting much out of this one. Please show me something about Jesus here. Or give me some instruction or teaching. Show me how you want to encourage me, or give me hope from this. Speak to me through this verse." I have added, sometimes, "I dare you," because, like you, I find many Bible passages hard to understand at first.

In the case of the non-muzzled ox, we have it easy, because the apostle Paul showed how this verse instructs followers of Jesus.

> For it is written in the law of Moses, **Do not muzzle an ox while it treads out grain.** Is God really concerned with oxen? Or isn't He really saying it for us? Yes, this is written for us, because he who plows ought to plow in hope, and he who threshes should do so in hope of sharing the crop. If we have sown spiritual things for you, is it too much if we reap material benefits from you? If others have this right to receive benefits from you, don't we even more? However, we have not made use of this right; instead we endure everything so that we will not hinder the gospel of Christ. Don't you know that those who perform the temple services eat the food from the temple, and those who serve at the altar share in the offerings of the altar? In the same way, the Lord has commanded that those who preach the gospel should earn their living by the gospel. (1Cor 9:9-14, HCSB)

It was written originally about oxen. It taught the people of Israel to be kind, and even generous, with the animals that worked for them. It taught them that the harvest was to be shared – even with the animals. Paul sees an enduring principle here that applies to preachers of the gospel. Paul writes, "Is God really concerned with oxen?" Asking questions is always a good way to begin to understand the underlying principle. I'm sure God *is* concerned about oxen, but if we treat our oxen well, shouldn't we also treat people well? If we are generous with the animals who make the physical harvest possible, what should we do with the people who make the spiritual harvest possible? Paul concludes: "Those who preach the gospel should earn their living by the gospel."

This is not *directly* about Jesus. But it is instruction for those of us who are trying to follow him. It tells us that if we are Jesus followers, we should support those who are called to teach the Bible. You may not have oxen, but if you are a Christian you probably have a pastor, or at least some leader or ministry from where you get spiritual leadership and solid biblical teaching. This passage about oxen doesn't apply to oxen any more (unless you own them, and use them to tread out grain). But it still applies to our lives as Jesus-followers. We are still supposed to share generously with those who help us spiritually.

By the way, of course I am one of those that preaches the gospel, and I know this passage applies to me, and to my ministry. But I don't share it here as a covert way of asking for money. I have no problem doing that directly: If the Lord leads you to, then give. Use the information at the end of this book. If you don't feel led to give, then don't. It's all between you and Him.

Can we move on now? The reason I used this passage is because the New Testament serves it up for us on a platter. It's a clear example of how we can use even what appear to be silly ancient laws to hear what God wants to teach us.

THE POINT:

The Bible was inspired by God. It is God's Word to humanity. The purpose of the entire Bible, both Old and New Testaments, is to help us get to know Jesus better, and to provide us with instruction, training, teaching, correction, encouragement, endurance, hope; and to equip us for good works.

PART II: HOW TO UNDERSTAND THE BIBLE BETTER

7

An Overview

We've examined a lot of background about the Bible that should give you more confidence in it. In addition, I've given you the first step in "seeing the whole elephant." We need to remember that the purpose of the entire Bible is to reveal Jesus to us. We read it so we can know him, and know him better, and follow him more fully. We examined that in the last chapter.

If you haven't figured it out yet, I am writing from the belief that the Bible is inspired by God, and is reliable and authoritative. In other words, it never fails to communicate God's message to us, and if we call ourselves Christians, we must believe what it says, and live by it. We don't get to pick and choose which parts we like. The goal of Bible study and interpretation is not so that we can gain ammunition to defend our point of view, or attack the views of another. We don't read the Bible in order to make it conform to our world view. Instead, we seek to understand it, and when we do, to submit to it, even when it challenges our pre-existing world view.

Mostly, the Bible is pretty straightforward and easy to understand. However, there are certainly parts of it that can be difficult, especially if you don't know how to approach it. It doesn't help that many people do strange things with the Bible, and seem to lose their common sense when it comes to it.

Therefore, in the next few chapters, I want to teach you some general principles and practices that will help you understand the Bible properly, and keep you from getting confused by the many people who do not get it. In theology, these principles and practices are called "**hermeneutics**" (pronounced: "her-mah-new-tiks"). Mostly, they represent a simple, common-sense approach to the Bible. The basic principles of hermeneutics have been accepted by serious Bible scholars for centuries. Vast numbers of books have been written on the subject of hermeneutics, but here I will spell out the most important ones in simple terms. In later chapters, I will examine these rules in greater detail.

1. All scripture is inspired by God. First, this means that while the Bible comes to us *through* human authors, we believe that the true and ultimate author is God. Thus, for instance, the apostle Paul is not merely expressing personal opinions, but rather, passing along what the Holy Spirit inspired him to say. This is the basic position of historic Christianity, and we covered it already in chapter 6.

I do want to remark, however, that there is no point using: "The Bible says so!" with a person who does not believe that God inspired it. I, myself, do not care what the Book of Mormon says, because I do not think God inspired it. So if someone says, "You should live this way, because it's in the Book of Mormon," it means nothing to me. So, while *Christians* believe the Bible is God-inspired, simply quoting the Bible to people who do not believe it is probably fruitless. You might, however, consider sharing this book with such people, or at least offering some of the information found here.

2. Scripture passages should be interpreted in context. This simply means that we should pay attention to what the surrounding verses and chapters say. If we take single verses or sentences out of context, we can make the Bible (or any lengthy book, for that matter) say anything we like. For example, in one place in the Bible, there is a woman who is caught committing adultery. In another place Jesus says "Go, then and do the same." If you don't consider the context, you could put together these two verses, from two different locations, and justify adultery. Context almost always gives us clues about how we are to understand what we are reading.

One thing that may seem obvious is that we should also pay attention to what the verses we are focusing on actually say. Though it ought to be basic, I can't tell you how many people ignore what the verses actually say, and therefore arrive at wildly inaccurate interpretations.

In addition to the textual context, we must also pay attention to the historical and cultural context.

4. Scripture interprets scripture. What this means is that whenever possible, we use the Bible to shed meaning upon itself. For instance, if Paul, writing in the book of Romans, says that Joel 2:32 is referring to Jesus, than we should also accept that Joel 2:32 is a prediction of salvation through the name of the Messiah, who is Jesus Christ. In other words, in this instance, Romans helps us interpret Joel.

In addition, this means that **the Bible does not contradict itself.** We give God the benefit of the doubt by assuming that He knows what He inspired each Bible-writer to put down, and does not contradict His own messages. Practically then, if we can interpret a Bible passage either in a way that is harmonious with the rest of the Bible, or contradictory to it, we accept the interpretation that is in harmony. This is plain common sense, and we do this naturally with every other book we read. Often with the Bible, it is in closely examining the apparent contradictions that we find the most rewarding and profound meanings.

Another important implication of point #4 is that **clear Bible passages are used to help us understand obscure ones**. We do not build entire theologies based upon difficult and obscure passages. That is what *cults* do. Instead, the clear, easily understood sections of scripture guide us when we come to the obscure verses.

5. We must consider the *genre* of the passages we study. Some chapters are poetic. Others are historical narrative. Still others contain clear teaching. We need to bear in mind, that the style in which a given passage was written gives us clues for how to understand it properly. For instance, while we can learn lessons from historical narratives like the book of Judges, those lessons are not as clear as they are in a section like Romans, for example, which was written for the purpose of expressing doctrine. We will spend several chapters, later on, learning how to interpret various genres.

A PRACTICAL EXAMPLE OF HERMENEUTICS

Most of the time, we practice common-sense hermeneutics with every book we read. To help you see how these rules work, imagine that you are reading a book about penguins. The book has only one author. In an early chapter, the author writes that penguins, while they have wings, are flightless birds. In a later chapter, she describes penguins "soaring through the open blue." We have a choice about how to interpret this.

One option is to assume that the author has contradicted herself. This means that she is either wrong about penguins being flightless, or she is wrong about them soaring through the open blue. Normally, if we believed that the author really made such a blatant self-contradiction, we would reject the entire book, and consider it useless. A contradiction like that makes the author unreliable.

In almost any book we read, however, we reject the self-contradictory interpretation automatically. We assume that the author would not contradict herself so blatantly without explanation. So we assume that there must be some way to harmonize the interpretations.

If the text interprets itself, we take the clear statement about penguins being flightless, and applying it to the statement about "soaring", and realize that therefore, "soaring" cannot be describing flight. What about the genre? Is "soaring through the open blue" a technical description of flight, or is it a poetic metaphor? Obviously it is more the latter than the former. And is there a way to interpret these two statements in harmony? Certainly, if "soaring through the open blue" is a metaphor for swimming in the pristine blue waters of the Antarctic Ocean. If we read the sentence *in context*, we might even find an *explicit* reference to swimming.

Generally, we read a book about penguins correctly without even thinking about rules of interpretation. But because the Bible contains eternal truth that could affect us profoundly, we easily become distracted into over-analysis, and frequently forget to employ these simple rules.

For instance, suppose there was some reason that you deeply wanted to believe that penguins could fly. Understand that in this case, you are reading the book not in order to understand penguins better, but rather, to support your position about penguins flying. You could pull some sentences from the book *out of context* and say, "But the book says they have wings! What else are wings for, if not flying?" You could take the sentence about soaring through the open blue and add "They have wings, and they soar through the open blue. It's a no-brainer. Penguins fly." You could take a general principle, and point out that penguins are birds, and generally, birds fly. You might even point out that some species of penguin are migratory, and all the other migratory birds we know about migrate by flying.

If someone pointed out the fact that, according to the book, penguins swim, you might refute the argument by pointing out that swimming and flying are not mutually exclusive. Ducks and loons do both all the time.

My point is that even with something as straightforward as whether or not penguins fly, if you are willing to ignore these common sense rules for reading and interpreting books, you could construct an argument that: a) appears to be based upon an accurate book about penguins, and b) which sounds reasonable, c) which offers plausible explanations and arguments against the contrary position, but d) *is completely wrong*. All the while you are using *bad interpretation* to refute a clear sentence that says, "Penguins are flightless birds."

People do that with the Bible all the time.

For instance, for some reason, many people want to claim they are following the teachings of the Bible, and yet also want to engage in sex outside of marriage. They will point out that many people in the Bible had sex before marriage, or cheated on their spouse during marriage, or had sex with prostitutes. They might add that the message of the Bible is love and forgiveness, not condemnation.

These arguments a) appear to be based upon the Bible, and b) sound reasonable, c) offer plausible explanations and arguments against the contrary position, but d) *are completely wrong*. This is *bad interpretation* in an attempt to refute what the Bible *clearly says* about sex outside of marriage (usually called "sexual immorality" by English versions):

[18]Run from sexual immorality! (1Cor 6:18-HCSB)

[19]Now the works of the flesh are obvious: sexual immorality, moral impurity, promiscuity, [20]idolatry, sorcery, hatreds, strife, jealousy, outbursts of anger, selfish ambitions, dissensions, factions, [21]envy, drunkenness, carousing, and anything similar. I tell you about these things in advance — as I told you before — that those who practice such things will not inherit the kingdom of God. (Gal 5:19-21, HCSB)

[2]And walk in love, as the Messiah also loved us and gave Himself for us, a sacrificial and fragrant offering to God. [3]But sexual immorality and any impurity or greed should not even be heard of among you, as is proper for saints. (Eph 5:2-3, HCSB)

[14]Do not commit adultery. (Exod 20:14, HCSB)

Although the Bible records the fact that many people sinned, that does not mean that *we* should sin. Although the Bible tells us that forgiveness is available to everyone through Jesus Christ, it also maintains that we should avoid sinning, and sexual immorality is a sin (see verses above). The simple, straightforward rules of interpretation should help us avoid errors like this when reading the Bible.

THE POINT:

Rules of interpretation (hermeneutics) help us to properly understand the Bible. When we ignore them, we can easily fall into the trap of completely misreading the Bible and either ignoring what God says, or changing it.

8

Read the Bible in Context

Once we accept that the Bible is inspired by God, **the first common sense rule is this: READ THE BIBLE IN CONTEXT**

#1 Read it in Context with the Surrounding Verses

In the last chapter, I gave the example of a book about penguins. I asked you to imagine that the book said "Penguins are large, flightless birds," and later on had a section which described them soaring through the open blue. I then asked you to imagine how this could create an argument about whether or not penguins can fly.

The truth is that most people would read the book about penguins the way they read any other book, and they wouldn't even notice the "contradiction," **because they**

would read the book in context. In other words, they won't just take a few sentences of it here and there from different chapters, and use those to make broad declarations about penguins, or broad declarations about the book contradicting itself.

Instead of reading an isolated sentence about penguins soaring through the open blue, they will read the entire chapter in which the author describes SCUBA diving while she watches the penguins swim around her in the clear, blue sea. *In context*, "soaring through the open blue" is clearly about swimming, not flying.

The problem is, too many people read the Bible to use it in arguments, instead of reading it to get to know Jesus better. So, instead of reading it in context, they go searching for a verse, or a few verses, that seem to say what they want the Bible to say. Others want to discredit the Bible altogether, because they don't like what it says, so they go searching for isolated verses which sound like they contradict each other. But to someone who knows the Bible, all this usually sounds as silly as a person trying to use a well-researched book about penguins to prove that they fly.

This is one reason I so strongly recommend that you work your way around the Bible by reading in one book (say, Matthew) until you've read that whole book, and then pick another book (say, Romans) and do the same. Maybe you only have time to read a chapter, or just a few verses each day. That's fine. But read (however slowly) through one book at a time, moving from the beginning to the end of the book (I don't mean the whole Bible – I mean a book within the Bible).

If you don't, you will have great difficulty understanding what you read, because it won't be in context.

If everyone in the world who quotes the Bible did this, my blood pressure would be significantly lower. **Honestly, I'd like to say that "Read the Bible in Context" is the first, second and third rule of common sense Bible understanding.**

Let me give you an example of context. Suppose a friend of mine claims to be a Christian, but he watches pornographic movies, and visits nude-bars. He sees nothing wrong with doing these things. I might say to him, "You claim to follow Jesus. But the lust in your heart is something wrong, Jesus died to make it right. You shouldn't continue to feed your lust that way. Jesus is calling you to repent."

Suppose he replies to me (quoting the Bible) "Jesus said, 'Don't judge others!'"

Do you know the context for those words of Jesus? He said it in Matthew 7:1, during the famous "Sermon on the Mount." Do you know what *else* he said in that very same sermon? He said he had not come to abolish the law, but to fulfill it, and anyone who relaxed the standards of the law was in trouble (Matthew 5:17-20). He also said lust was wrong (Matthew 5:27-30).

In fact, let's look at the *context* where Jesus told us not to judge:

> 1"Do not judge, so that you won't be judged. 2For with the judgment you use, you will be judged, and with the measure you use, it will be measured to you. 3Why do you look at the speck in your brother's eye but don't notice the log in your own eye? 4Or

> how can you say to your brother, 'Let me take the speck out of your eye,' and look, there's a log in your eye?
>
> 5Hypocrite! First take the log out of your eye, and then you will see clearly to take the speck out of your brother's eye.
>
> 6Don't give what is holy to dogs or toss your pearls before pigs, or they will trample them with their feet, turn, and tear you to pieces. (Matt 7:1-6, HCSB)

The context of "do not judge" is the whole Sermon on the Mount, as I mentioned. In that context, there is simply no way that my friend can defend his activities as righteous and OK. The context declares that lust is wrong, so "judge not," clearly cannot mean: "Lust is OK."

"Judge not" does not make him free to do whatever he wants. Also, it doesn't have to stop me from confronting him. Even in this closer context of Matthew 7:1-6, we can see that it is not as simple as "don't judge." Jesus actually says we should examine ourselves first, and then we will be able to help someone else who has a problem. He says we should recognize that the same standards apply to us, as well as the other person (verse 2). In other words, we need to be humble, and recognize our own faults, before we approach someone else to help them with their problem (verse 5). But Jesus' words here (in context) assume that *we should still approach the person*, once we are appropriately humble (verse 5).

The last sentence gives us some additional information. Jesus seems to be saying that it is pointless to "judge" where the person is not interested in receiving it. It's like giving jewelry to pigs – you are wasting your time. Such people will not appreciate the precious words of God, and instead will get angry at you. In context then, "Do not judge," means:

- Be humble, and willing to acknowledge your own faults before you talk to someone else about his. Recognize that the same standard you apply to someone else also applies to you.

- You should still talk to the other person, once you are appropriately humble.

- Do not bother to judge those who are proud, unwilling to admit to their faults, or uninterested in what the Bible has to say. One thing I take away from this, is that it is pointless to try to get people who do not want to be Christian to stop sinning.

There is more to be said about this passage, and more we can learn from other Bible-reading techniques, but merely reading the context makes this often-misused quote much more clear and understandable.

Let me give you another example of reading in textual context. A friend of mine used to smoke marijuana all the time. He quoted this verse to me:

> 4For everything created by God is good, and nothing should be rejected if it is received with thanksgiving, 5since it is sanctified by the word of God and by prayer. (1Tim 4:4-5, HCSB)

He said, "Marijuana is a plant, created by God. It should not be rejected. We are supposed to receive it with thanksgiving."

You could apply this to all sorts of things, actually. I believe opium and cocaine are also plant-products. God created these plants, so shouldn't we receive them with thanksgiving? Of course, there are many, many poisonous plants also created by God. Should we also consume them with thanksgiving? Where does this line of thinking end?

The answer is that if we **read the context**, it ends before it even starts. Let me give you the greater textual context:

> 1Now the Spirit explicitly says that in later times some will depart from the faith, paying attention to deceitful spirits and the teachings of demons, 2through the hypocrisy of liars whose consciences are seared. 3They forbid marriage and demand abstinence from foods that God created to be received with gratitude by those who believe and know the truth. 4For everything created by God is good, and nothing should be rejected if it is received with thanksgiving, 5since it is sanctified by the word of God and by prayer. (1Tim 4:1-5, HCSB)

We can see that Paul is writing to Timothy about certain false teachers who forbid marriage and demand abstinence from certain kinds of foods. *In context*, the scripture is saying that marriage is created by God, and it is good, and that food is also created by God, and is also good. We shouldn't feel bad about wanting to get married. We shouldn't feel bad about eating bacon or shrimp. We don't have to obey the "Kosher regulations" anymore – we receive all food with thanksgiving. In context, you see, this has nothing to do with either drugs or poison.

If you do not know how the verses you are reading fit in with the surrounding verses, then you cannot properly understand the verses you are reading.

#2 Read the Bible in Cultural/Historical Context

The most important thing is to read the context in the Bible itself, as described above. However, the historical situation and the cultural context are also tremendously important. We have already walked through how we got the Bible. It was not dictated out of thin air, into thin air. God inspired people to speak and write about the situations they faced. Those situations took place at real times in history, and in real places. **In order to understand what a Bible passage means to us today, we need to understand what it meant to those who first heard it. To get that understanding, we need to know the historical and cultural context.**

For instance, let's talk once more about when Jesus said, "Do not judge." Would it make a difference whether the people he was speaking to were inclined to be judgmental? Would it matter *what* they were inclined to make their judgments about? Of course.

If we knew something about 1st Century Judaism, we would realize that the Jews Jesus was speaking to were generally very religious and legalistic about *silly little rules*. In fact, we would find out that often times, they condemned others for not following *man-made rules*, rules that had nothing to do with what God actually said. For instance, Exodus 20:8-11 says to remember the Sabbath, and keep it holy. By the time of Jesus, the Jews had made up an extensive list of rules which detailed exactly how they were supposed to keep the Sabbath holy. The problem was, those rules did not come from God, or the Bible. The Jewish rules were made up by human beings, *and added to* the inspired word of God.

So, the Jews said, you can only walk a certain number of steps on the Sabbath. You can do *this*, but not *that*. The Jews **judged others** based on how well they followed these kinds of petty, man-made rules. But those rules didn't even come from God in the first place.

It is to people like this that Jesus says: "do not judge." This is why Jesus talks about logs and splinters in the eye. The Jews were concerned about how well others followed man-made rules, while they ignored what the Bible said about the Messiah, and faith, and real sin, and forgiveness, and relationship with God.

So, the "log in your own eye" that Jesus refers to is the tendency to completely ignore Jesus himself, while focusing on petty little things that aren't even in the Bible.

Knowing the cultural/historical context, we now understand that Jesus isn't saying that we should not tell a fellow Christian that lust is sinful. **He is saying that we should keep our priorities straight, and not judge others based upon meaningless, petty, or man-made rules.** Like the Jews of Jesus' time, some Christians have made up rules – you must dress a certain way, or avoid certain kinds of movies, or avoid drinking even one glass of wine with dinner, or listen only to certain kinds of music. These are specks that some people try to pick out of the eyes of others. But the log in the eye is this: How do you respond to Jesus? How do you respond to his message of sin and redemption?

Do you see how the historical context can help you understand a passage more fully? **If you do not understand what a Bible verse meant to those who first heard it, you**

cannot understand what God is saying to you through that verse today.

Now, I don't want to scare you. In much of the Bible, it's pretty easy to see what the verse meant to those who first heard it. For instance, when God said "Do not murder," to the Israelites, it meant the same thing as "Do not murder" means to us today. In large portions of the Bible, the historical/cultural context does not change the meaning of the words. But if you find yourself puzzled by something, or if you hear people interpreting a verse in a way that makes you wonder, please investigate the historical and cultural context.

People often ask me, "Tom, where do we find out historical and cultural information like that?" The bad news is, there isn't just one easy source for it. But the good news is, I was once asking the same question, and over the years, I have learned a lot.

If I was starting out, the first thing I would do is get a good, high-quality study Bible. I highly recommend *The ESV Study Bible*. There are helpful notes and commentary at the bottom of each page. Not all of the commentary is about the cultural background, of course, but often there are useful notes there about the culture and history.

You might also google "Manners and Customs of Bible Times." There are several good resources that will show up. Unfortunately, some people create these resources with a theological axe to grind, so to speak. For example, I was personally disappointed by the *Inter-Varsity Press Bible Background Commentary*. Generally, the older the publishing date, the less biased one way or the other it is likely to be. *Manners and Customs of Bible Times* by Fred Wright is available online for free. I've used that from time to time, and found it very helpful. *Eerdman's Handbook to the Bible* is another good general resource, as is *Halley's Bible Handbook*. I will say more about these resources in *Chapter 19: Practical Tools*.

It will take time to work your way through these resources. That's OK, you have your whole life to study the Bible. It is also helpful to listen to sermons. Many pastors, like me, have spent a great deal of time learning this stuff. Pay attention to the preachers who explain the historical and cultural context, because, as I've been saying, it's important. If you think you might forget it, make notes of the things you think are significant. Over time, you will build up your own body of knowledge about Bible history and culture.

THE POINT:

Read the Bible in context. Understand that each book within the Bible was written as a whole, and read it the same way. Don't focus on one verse while excluding the verses around it. Also, read the Bible in *historical and cultural* context. It is impossible to properly understand what the Bible means without understanding these two types of context.

9

Scripture Interprets Scripture

After context, the next most important rule for understanding the Bible is this: **Scripture interprets Scripture**. In other words, very often, some parts of the Bible help us to understand other parts.

Let's go back to our book about penguins. The context helped us understand that "soaring through the open blue" did not mean flying. But there was another way to know that the author did not intend us to believe that penguins could fly. It is this: ***the author said so***, earlier in the book. She wrote: "Penguins are large, flightless birds." That statement is very clear – it tells us penguins are birds that cannot fly. Therefore, when we look at the second statement (the one about soaring through the open blue), we already know that it must not mean flying.

Do you see what happened there? First, we assumed that the author would not contradict herself. Next, we used one part of the book to clarify our understanding of another part that was more obscure. Generally, we do this with almost every book we read. We should do it with the Bible as well.

Therefore, **we should use the clear parts of the Bible to help us understand the more difficult things**. In addition, we assume that **the Bible does not contradict itself**. Where it appears to, we look for a way to resolve the contradiction.

Let's put all this together with an example. The New Testament teaches very clearly that we cannot earn our salvation. We are forgiven for our sins, restored to a healthy, joyous relationship with God, and given eternal life, only because of the work Jesus has already done for us. We receive those gifts only by God's grace, through trusting Jesus Christ, not through any works that we do. Here are some verses which teach this clearly. I've italicized parts of them, for emphasis:

> We too all previously lived among them in our fleshly desires, carrying out the inclinations of our flesh and thoughts, and we were by nature children under wrath as the others were also. But God, who is rich in mercy, because of His great love that He had for us, made us alive with the Messiah even though we were dead in trespasses. *You are saved by grace!* Together with Christ Jesus He also raised us up and seated us in the heavens, so that in the coming ages He might display the immeasurable riches of *His grace* through His kindness to us in Christ Jesus. *For you are saved by grace through faith,*

and this is not from yourselves; it is God's gift — *not from works*, so that no one can boast. (Eph 2:3-9, HCSB)

Where then is boasting? It is excluded. By what kind of law? By one of works? No, on the contrary, by a law of faith. *For we conclude that a man is justified by faith apart from the works of the law.* (Rom 3:27-28, HCSB)

He has saved us and called us with a holy calling, *not according to our works, but according to His own purpose and grace,* which was given to us in Christ Jesus before time began. This has now been made evident through the appearing of our Savior Christ Jesus, who has abolished death and has brought life and immortality to light through the gospel. (2Tim 1:9-10, HCSB)

He saved us — not by works of righteousness that we had done, but according to His mercy, through the washing of regeneration and renewal by the Holy Spirit. He poured out this Spirit on us abundantly through Jesus Christ our Savior, *so that having been justified by His grace*, we may become heirs with the hope of eternal life. (Titus 3:5-7, HCSB)

Yet we know that no one is justified by the works of the law but by faith in Jesus Christ. And we have believed in Christ Jesus, so that we might be justified by faith in Christ *and not by the works of the law*, because by the works of the law no human being will be justified. (Gal 2:16-17, ESV)

This is all quite clear, and I could add dozens of other verses which say the same thing. But now, consider these *other* verses (again, I've italicized parts for emphasis):

But when you pray, go into your room, close the door and pray to your Father, who is unseen. Then *your Father, who sees what is done in secret, will reward you.* (Matt 6:6)

What good will it be for a man if he gains the whole world, yet forfeits his soul? Or what can a man give in exchange for his soul? For the Son of Man is going to come in his Father's glory with his angels, and *then he will reward each person according to what he has done.* (Matthew 16:26-27)

But love your enemies, do good to them, and lend to them without expecting to get anything back. *Then your reward will be great,* and you will be sons of the Most High, because he is kind to the ungrateful and wicked. (Luke 6:35)

Serve wholeheartedly, as if you were serving the Lord, not men, *because you know that the Lord will reward everyone for whatever good he does,* whether he is slave or free. (Ephesians 6:7-8)

So we have these many, clear verses telling us that salvation is a gracious gift, not a reward for good works. But then we have these other verses telling us that God will reward us according to our works. ***Isn't this a contradiction?***

No. Not any more than "soaring through the open blue" is a contradiction of "penguins are large, flightless birds."

In the book on penguins, we gave the author the benefit of the doubt. We started off by assuming there was no contradiction. So, we looked for a way to harmonize the two statements, and we allowed what was clear to shed light on what was more obscure.

Let's do the same for the Bible. Clearly, salvation is not a reward – it is a gracious gift of God that can only be received

97

in humble faith, not by earning it. Those verses are crystal clear. Now, let's think about the other verses, the ones that talk about rewards. Do any of them say that *salvation* is the reward they are talking about? No. So, doesn't it make sense to assume that salvation is one thing, and rewards are something else? (That was a rhetorical question. Of course it does).

The problem is resolved then, when we see that the Bible makes a distinction between salvation, and other rewards that are *not* salvation. This is one way in which scripture interprets scripture.

There's another thing to keep in mind with "Scripture interprets Scripture." The New Testament directly quotes and explains the Old Testament on numerous occasions. We saw an example of that in chapter six, when we looked at 1 Corinthians 9:9-14. Those verses explained how we should understand Deuteronomy 25:4 ("Do not muzzle an ox while it treads out grain").

For this reason, it is very helpful to have a Bible which contains *cross references*. When Paul writes the part about oxen, he only says that it comes from the Law (which, to most New Testament writers, usually means the Torah, which is the first five books of the Bible). However, Paul does not give us a chapter or verse reference, for the very good reason that chapters and verse markings weren't put into the Bible until more than a thousand years after Paul wrote. So, how did I find out that Paul was quoting Deuteronomy 25:4?

In my Bible, right after the words, there is a little, superscript "c" like this[c]. If I look at the bottom of the page in my Bible, there is another little superscript "c," corresponding to the one in the text. It says, "ᶜ9:9 Dt 25:4". "9:9" tells me that the note is referring to that chapter and verse on the page I am reading – in this case, 1 Corinthians 9:9. "Dt 25:4" is an abbreviation for "Deuteronomy chapter twenty-five, verse four." I looked up that verse, and sure enough, it says: "Do not muzzle an ox while it treads out grain."

If you start paying attention to cross references, and looking them up, you will find that your Bible reading becomes deeper and more meaningful. Cross references will help you see how some parts of the Bible guide you in understanding others.

THE POINT:

If we pay attention, the Bible will help us understand itself. If we come across something that seems like a contradiction, instead of assuming it is, we should investigate alternative ways to interpret the "contradicting" verses. We will benefit from using a Bible with *cross references* to help allow clear verses to shed light on obscure ones.

10

Genre: Introduction

We've considered the origins of the Bible. We've established its historicity and reliability. In the past few chapters we began to learn a few simple rules for reading the Bible and understanding it properly. The first rule was to *read the Bible in context*. It is rarely helpful to read a verse or two, without understanding what came before or after it. In addition, we need to read the Bible in its historical and cultural context. In other words, we ought to understand what it really meant to the people who first heard it or read it, in their culture, before we will be able to properly apply it to our own lives. We have also learned the rule of "scripture interprets scripture," that is, to let clear parts of the Bible help us in understanding things that are less clear.

In this chapter, I want to look at another important principle of reading the Bible: Genre.

There are many different kinds of literature (genres) in the Bible. We need to be aware of them, and consider the writing style, before we try to apply the Bible directly to our lives. We have already learned that the Bible is actually sixty-six different books, written by dozens of different people from dozens of different walks of life. Some parts of the Bible are **laws**. Others are records of **family history**. There is also a great deal of official "court" or **government history**. There are **genealogies** – lists and records of family names. Some of the Bible is prophecy, and there are at least **two different kinds of prophecy**. There is a great deal of **poetry and song** in the Bible. The book of Proverbs is mostly made up of, well, *proverbs* – wise sayings. There are four **accounts of the ministry and teachings of Jesus** (we call them "**gospels**.") Within Jesus' teachings are a unique kind of literature called **parables**. In many of the books, there are sections containing fairly straightforward **teaching** about Jesus and how to follow him. A lot of teaching is found in letters written by the apostles.

I have just listed at least ten major genres, or types of writing, found in the Bible. We need to pay attention to these when we read the Bible. We will need to read poetry with a very different approach than we use when we read one of Paul's letters to Jesus-followers. When we read a historical section, we ought to treat it differently than we treat a prophecy.

Imagine the song "*Silent Night.*" Like many Christmas songs, it has been arranged in many different ways, and played by many different groups and performing artists. Think of it being played instrumentally, by an orchestra. You've probably heard it that way. Now, imagine how it sounds sung by a full choir, with no instruments at all. It's the same song. The same music is being conveyed, and yet, it sounds very different. Now, hear a twangy, country-western singer singing *Silent Night*. Next, try to imagine someone singing it as a kind of operatic solo. Picture it done to swing-rhythm. Now imagine it as "muzak" or "elevator music," played at the mall. Think of a rendition of the song by a 1940's "big band." Hear it done by Reggae artists.

All of these are the same song, conveying the same "musical message." And yet each style and performance conveys that same "musical message" in a very different way. We can appreciate some of those ways better than others, but it all goes back to the same composer, the same basic set of notes, the same lyrics.

This is kind of how the Bible is. Sometimes, God conveyed his message through the life of an old man, or a young princess. Sometimes, he sent it through laws that helped people at that time understand him better. At other times, God's message came through prophets, or teachers, or letter writers, kings, or musicians. Sometimes, it is hard to recognize as the same message, because three-thousand year-old laws require more work to understand than clearly written letters from more than a thousand years later. But the messages about God, human beings and relationships are consistent throughout the Bible. As with *Silent Night*, though the "performances" are widely varied, the basic underlying message is the same. Different musicians may play the music, different instruments may create it, but at the same time, the music is, and always was, the product of the original composer.

It is important to realize that even when a book of the Bible is predominantly one genre (say, history) it might still contain sections that are written in other genres. For instance, 2 Samuel is mostly a historical book. But it also contains some poetry – a lament that David wrote for the fallen warriors Saul and Jonathan.

For the next few chapters, we'll consider the main genres found in the Bible, and what each one means for how to understand what the Bible is saying. This book is meant to be useful for regular people with jobs and kids and "to do lists," so I will not go overboard here. Think of it as a quick and useful way to help you understand the genres of the Bible, not as a comprehensive guide.

One other thing is very important. **Considering genre works together with considering context, and with "scripture interprets scripture." We don't *either* look at context *or* at genre. We don't *either* consider genre, *or* what other parts of the Bible say about the same subject. We do it *all*, and that gives us a much better understanding of what the Bible is truly saying.**

We will briefly consider nine major genres in the upcoming chapters.

THE POINT:

The genre of a verse, passage or book in the Bible should influence how we understand it. Sometimes we are not supposed to take what the passage says literally; sometimes we are. Understanding genre will help us avoid mistakes and teach us to interpret the Bible in better ways.

11

Genre: Teaching

Let's start with the "teaching" genre. We can learn lessons from any kind of genre. But the "teaching" genre is sometimes easier, because it presents material in a straightforward way. Here is an example of teaching:

5"Whenever you pray, you must not be like the hypocrites, because they love to pray standing in the synagogues and on the street corners to be seen by people. I assure you: They've got their reward! 6But when you pray, go into your private room, shut your door, and pray to your Father who is in secret. And your Father who sees in secret will reward you. 7When you pray, don't babble like the idolaters, since they imagine they'll be heard for their many words. 8Don't be like them, because your Father knows the things you need before you ask Him.

> ₉"Therefore, you should pray like this: Our Father in heaven, Your name be honored as holy. ₁₀Your kingdom come. Your will be done on earth as it is in heaven.₁₁Give us today our daily bread.₁₂And forgive us our debts, as we also have forgiven our debtors.₁₃And do not bring us into temptation, but deliver us from the evil one. (Matt 6:4-12, HCSB)

Jesus was the one who said this. Think about what he means when he says: "When you pray, don't babble like the idolaters, since they imagine they'll be heard for their many words. Don't be like them, because your Father knows the things you need before you ask Him." What's the message here?

The message is that we cannot motivate God to action simply by using a lot of words. It means we can trust that God knows what we need, so when we pray, it is best to be simple and straightforward. **In other words, it means what it says**. That is a characteristic of the teaching genre. There is no "hidden" message here. It is not an allegory or a story. It is a straightforward presentation of ideas or instructions.

Now, as a teacher of the Bible, I can probably find a lot to say about these verses. In fact, I once preached for seven weeks, just on verses 9-14. But I didn't come up with anything that wasn't already there. I just found ways to help us think about these things and make them practical. For instance, "Our Father" shows us that we should view God as a good father, one who is ready to listen and willing to take on our burdens. It is the attitude we should take toward God, particularly as we approach Him in prayer.

So, I can "flesh out" what "Our Father" means for us when we pray. But the meaning isn't hidden, and it isn't an allegory. Good preachers merely help people to make the meaning of Bible teachings relevant and applicable to everyday life.

Let me give you some teaching that is a little bit harder to understand:

> 11You were also circumcised in Him with a circumcision not done with hands, by putting off the body of flesh, in the circumcision of the Messiah.12Having been buried with Him in baptism, you were also raised with Him through faith in the working of God, who raised Him from the dead.13And when you were dead in trespasses and in the uncircumcision of your flesh, He made you alive with Him and forgave us all our trespasses.14He erased the certificate of debt, with its obligations, that was against us and opposed to us, and has taken it out of the way by nailing it to the cross. (Col 2:11-14, HCSB)

This is still a straightforward presentation of ideas. The apostle Paul, in a letter to the Colossians, is teaching something about what the Messiah (Christ) has done for us. It can be confusing, however, because we aren't necessarily familiar with all the concepts he is using to present his teaching. We might need to learn what he means by "circumcision," and "flesh." We don't always use the word "trespasses," and it might help us to look that up somewhere. But once we have learned these things, the meaning is pretty clear. We can see that through the Messiah, we are counted as dead to sin, and alive to God. Our trespasses (sins) are forgiven. This happened through the work of Jesus Christ on the cross. All this is basically exactly what it says.

There are two more important things about the teaching genre.

First, if you end up with a meaning that is almost opposite to what the text obviously appears to say, you are probably doing something wrong. Let's go back to Matthew 6:7-8, and I'll give you an example of doing it wrong.

> 7When you pray, don't babble like the idolaters, since they imagine they'll be heard for their many words.8Don't be like them, because your Father knows the things you need before you ask Him.

*[How **not** to interpret teaching parts of the Bible]:*

Jesus does not want us to be like the idolaters. Idols are nothing – mere pieces of metal, wood or stone. So, of course no matter how many words you say, an idol is never going to hear you. So all those words are wasted on idols. Instead, use your many words to pray to God. Of course you can babble on when you pray to God – when you are talking to God, he hears you, so the fancier and more wordy your prayers, the better.

Especially if I like to pray long, wordy prayers, I might be tempted to approach it like that. My interpretation would help justify my actions. It sounds pretty good, if I do say so myself. But it is bad Bible interpretation. One clue that I have done a poor job, is that my interpretation *is almost the opposite of what the text appears to say*. In a different genre, that may be legitimate, *but in the teaching genre*, beware of interpretations that seem to say the opposite of what the text says.

Now, I might find legitimate ways to examine what Jesus said and make it more practical to everyday life. I might dwell on how God is indeed not an idol, and he does indeed hear me when I pray. I might consider how wonderful it is that he knows what I need even before I ask, so that when I do ask, I can have a peaceful, trustful attitude. Those things do not say something different than what the verses say – they merely "flesh it out" a little bit. Those thoughts help make it more real to me. That is a legitimate way to understand the teaching parts of the Bible.

A second thing to remember is that **because teaching genre is mostly quite clear, we use the teaching parts of the Bible to help us understand other parts that aren't as clear.**

For instance, suppose we read in a narrative part of the Bible (a part that records events) about a person who prays a long, wordy prayer, going on and on, after which God answers the prayer. That narrative/historical part of the Bible is not telling us that God answered the prayer *because* the person used so many words. It is merely recording what happened, not giving us specific, clear guidance about prayer. On the other hand, in Matthew 6:7-8, Jesus *is* giving us specific, clear guidance about prayer. Since that is so clear, we can look at the other passage, and say, "God did not answer the person *because* he used so many words. In fact, considering what Jesus says, God answered the long, wordy prayer *in spite of the fact* that it was long and wordy."

What I am saying is that generally, the teaching genre helps us understand what the other genres are saying.

This makes the teaching genre very, very important. Most of the New Testament is written in the teaching genre.

THE POINT:

The Teaching genre expresses truth in a straightforward, clear way. It is usually fairly easy to understand. Where possible, we should use the teaching parts of scripture to help us understand more confusing genres.

12

Genre: Narrative

Many parts of the Bible tell us about *events that took place*. This genre is called "historical," or "narrative." Many Old Testament books contain narrative: Genesis, Joshua, Judges, Esther, Ruth, 1-2 Samuel, 1-2 Kings, 1-2 Chronicles, Ezra and Nehemiah are all predominately narrative. In addition, many other books have major sections that are written as narrative: Exodus, Numbers, Isaiah and Jeremiah.

Of course, Matthew, Mark, Luke and John contain a lot of narrative, besides also recording the teachings of Jesus. The book of Acts is mostly narrative.

Some of the narrative is written in the first person ("*I* did this, and then that happened"). The majority of it, however, is written in the third person (*"He* did this, and then that happened.")

Historical/narrative is the record, or "story," of real people and real events. As we learned previously, there is no reason to doubt the Bible when it gives us historical narrative, and plenty of reasons to believe it. So we read it as a record of something that actually happened. We can get spiritual lessons from historical sections of the Bible, but we ought to keep in mind that history isn't primarily a parable, or an allegory – it is a record of what happened. Because of that, history isn't always ideal. King David committed adultery and murder. The record of those sinful actions is **not** a *teaching*, telling us that it is okay for leaders to do such things. **It is simply telling us what David actually did, not what *we* ought to do, or even what *he* ought to have done.** In the historical situations, we look at how God dealt with people and nations in the events of their lives, and learn how God may deal with us at times. We look at mistakes and failures, and learn lessons concerning what we ought to avoid. We look at victories, and learn how to trust God to work through us. We see God's faithful love at work in the past, and take encouragement from it.

For instance, in the book of 1 Samuel, we have a narrative telling us that David was anointed to be king when he was just a teenager. The narrative goes on for many, many chapters, telling us of the various struggles, trials, triumphs, and defeats that David experienced after that. It tells us how David did not actually become king for another fifteen years or so after God chose him. This is not a direct teaching. But we can receive encouragement from the narrative. We can take note, and realize that sometimes God's plans take a long time to come to fruition. Sometimes, even when God is working, there is a lot of trial and struggle involved. The difficulties do not mean God has abandoned us. They do not mean that his will has been thwarted.

On the other hand, 1 Samuel is a record of what happened, not a direct teaching. So, we can't say, based on this part of the Bible, that God's plans must *always* involve a lot of struggle, and take a lot of time to come to fruition. That's how it worked for David, so we shouldn't despair if it happens to us also. We should be encouraged to trust God, even if his promises seem slow in coming to pass. But we can't say, based upon the narrative of 1 Samuel, that it should *always* be like that.

Narrative is one of the places where the Bible is frequently misinterpreted. For instance, many people of faith in Old Testament times kept slaves, and the Bible sometimes mentions that. **But the fact that Bible narratives record that people had slaves is not at all the same as a *teaching* that slavery is legitimate, or acceptable to God.**

If you run into someone who wants to discredit the Bible, chances are they will bring up either slavery or polygamy, and say something like: "The Bible says slavery (or polygamy) is OK. It's there, in the Bible."

But it isn't. What *is* in the Bible is an accurate, unvarnished record of what people actually did, and how they behaved. The parts about slavery and polygamy are found in the narrative sections, and the laws (we'll talk more about laws later on). There is no *direct teaching* that endorses either slavery or polygamy.

This is one reason it is so important to understand genre.

There is a special type of narrative that I want to mention. That is: **Genealogy.** There are a number of places throughout the Bible that contain extensive lists of family, clan and tribal records. I admit, this is the hardest genre (or rather, sub-genre) for me. Lists of families and names just don't seem to bring me a lot of spiritual benefit. But every so often, God blesses me through one of the genealogical lists in the Bible.

For instance, look at the genealogy of Jesus, listed in Matthew 1:1-17 (skim it quickly for now, if you like).

> 1The historical record of Jesus Christ, the Son of David, the Son of Abraham:
> 2Abraham fathered Isaac, Isaac fathered Jacob, Jacob fathered Judah and his brothers,3Judah fathered Perez and Zerah by Tamar, Perez fathered Hezron, Hezron fathered Aram,4Aram fathered Amminadab, Amminadab fathered Nahshon, Nahshon fathered Salmon,5Salmon fathered Boaz by Rahab, Boaz fathered Obed by Ruth, Obed fathered Jesse,6and Jesse fathered King David.
> Then David fathered Solomon by Uriah's wife,7Solomon fathered Rehoboam, Rehoboam fathered Abijah, Abijah fathered Asa,8Asa fathered Jehoshaphat, Jehoshaphat fathered Joram, Joram fathered Uzziah,9Uzziah fathered Jotham, Jotham fathered Ahaz, Ahaz fathered Hezekiah,10Hezekiah fathered Manasseh, Manasseh fathered Amon, Amon fathered Josiah,11and Josiah fathered Jechoniah and his brothers at the time of the exile to Babylon.
> 12Then after the exile to Babylon Jechoniah fathered Shealtiel, Shealtiel fathered Zerubbabel,13Zerubbabel fathered Abiud, Abiud

> fathered Eliakim, Eliakim fathered Azor,14Azor
> fathered Zadok, Zadok fathered Achim, Achim
> fathered Eliud,15Eliud fathered Eleazar, Eleazar
> fathered Matthan, Matthan fathered Jacob,16and
> Jacob fathered Joseph the husband of Mary, who
> gave birth to Jesus who is called the Messiah. (Matt
> 1:1-16, HCSB)

It makes you sleepy just reading it, right? However, when you start looking up these names, it becomes more interesting. It turns out that many of the physical ancestors of Joseph (in other words, Jesus' earthly family) and even of Mary (she was related to Joseph) were scoundrels. Two of the women were prostitutes! Yet we see that God gave them grace, and used them anyway. He removed their shame and through them, brought the Messiah into the world. I have found similar lessons in other genealogies. The trick is to look up the people listed, and see what you can learn about them.

THE POINT:

Narrative is valuable because it shows us how real people of faith lived, followed God, made mistakes, and went through difficult times. We can learn a lot from the narrative accounts of people in the Bible. We can receive encouragement and hope from seeing how God dealt with the lives of his people in the past. Even so, we should be careful to understand that narrative records what actually happened. It is not necessarily a teaching telling us that we should do the same.

13

Genre: Prophecy

Huge portions of the Bible contain the proclamations of various prophets.

There are several variations to the genre of prophecy. Of course what everyone usually thinks about when they hear the word "prophecy" is "a prediction of the future." That is one kind of Bible prophecy. I call it **"Predictive Prophecy."**

Reading predictive prophecy in the Bible is like looking at a range of distant mountains. From a distance, the mountains are silhouetted against the sky, and they look like they are all right next to each other in a giant cardboard cutout. However, when you get closer, you find that they are actually a series of ridges and peaks that go on for some time. The mountains aren't all lined up side by side, as it looks from a long way away. Some peaks are closer than others. Some that looked the same height are actually very different, but distance skewed our perspective when we were far away.

From the prophet's perspective (which is how it is written down in the Bible) it looks like all of the future will happen at one time. In reality, as you get closer, some things are fulfilled centuries before other things. So Isaiah talks about the destruction of Jerusalem (which happened 200 years after he prophesied), the return of the exiles from Babylon (which happened 70 years after that) the coming of the Messiah (which happened about 700 years after he prophesied) and the end of the world (which, as far as I know, hasn't happened yet), often all in the same proclamation. These prophecies about various times are jumbled in amongst each other. This is very important to remember when you read the prophetic portions of the Bible.

It also helps to know a little bit of history. A good study Bible (more on that later) will contain margin notes that tell you which prophecies have already been fulfilled in historical events. *Eerdman's Handbook to the Bible* is also helpful for that sort of thing.

Here is one example of predictive prophecy:
> 1Who has believed what we have heard?
> And who has the arm of the LORD been revealed to?
> 2He grew up before Him like a young plant
> and like a root out of dry ground.
> He didn't have an impressive form
> or majesty that we should look at Him,
> no appearance that we should desire Him.
> 3He was despised and rejected by men,
> a man of suffering who knew what sickness was.

He was like someone people turned away from;
He was despised, and we didn't value Him.
4Yet He Himself bore our sicknesses,
and He carried our pains;
but we in turn regarded Him stricken,
struck down by God, and afflicted.
5But He was pierced because of our transgressions,
crushed because of our iniquities;
punishment for our peace was on Him,
and we are healed by His wounds.
6We all went astray like sheep;
we all have turned to our own way;
and the LORD has punished Him
for the iniquity of us all.
7He was oppressed and afflicted,
yet He did not open His mouth.
Like a lamb led to the slaughter and like a sheep
silent before her shearers,
He did not open His mouth.
8He was taken away because of oppression and
judgment;
and who considered His fate?
For He was cut off from the land of the living;
He was struck because of my people's rebellion.
9They made His grave with the wicked
and with a rich man at His death,
although He had done no violence
and had not spoken deceitfully. (Isa 53:1-9, HCSB)

This prophecy describes Jesus, and what Jesus did when he died on the cross, even though the prophecy was made a good seven hundred years before he was born. No one recognized Jesus as the Son of God (verse 2). He was rejected by his own people (verse 3). Jesus took the punishment that should have been ours onto himself (verses 4-6), and his suffering brought us spiritual healing and peace with God. When Jesus was accused before the Jewish authorities, and then later, Pontius Pilate, he did not defend himself, but remained quiet, only answering when necessary, and not trying to save himself (verse 7). He was buried in the tomb of a rich man named Joseph of Arimathea (verse 9). This is just one of hundreds of predictive prophecies from the Bible that have already been fulfilled.

Prophecy also has a message to us in the present, regardless of the predictive element of it. I call this variation: **present prophecy**. Most of the prophets spoke to people about how to relate to God, and how God loves us, and longs to forgive and care for us. These words are still relevant today. So the comfort spoken to the exiles who would return to Jerusalem is also spoken to us, who seek peace and comfort in the Lord today. Again from Isaiah:

> 1 "Comfort, comfort My people,"
> says your God.
> 2 "Speak tenderly to Jerusalem,
> and announce to her
> that her time of forced labor is over,
> her iniquity has been pardoned,
> and she has received from the LORD's hand
> double for all her sins."
> 3 A voice of one crying out:
> Prepare the way of the LORD in the wilderness;
> make a straight highway for our God in the desert.
> 4 Every valley will be lifted up,
> and every mountain and hill will be leveled;
> the uneven ground will become smooth
> and the rough places, a plain. (Isaiah 40:1-4, HCSB)

This prophecy is a prediction about the coming of the Messiah, again fulfilled in Jesus. Jesus brought comfort (verse

1) and paid for our sins (verse 2). John the Baptist came before Jesus, preaching in the desert, preparing people for the beginning of his ministry (verse 3).

Even so, these verses still mean something to us, today, besides just the encouragement of knowing this was fulfilled in Jesus. **It is also fulfilled in Jesus in the present lives of those who follow him**. What I mean is, even today, as you read these verses, comfort can be spoken into your heart through Jesus. Even today, your sins are forgiven, paid for, by Jesus. Even today, the Holy Spirit speaks to us through these verses and says, "Prepare your heart and mind and life for the Lord. Let him fill up the valleys, the low, hurting and empty places in your life. Let him level the mountains: the pride, the sins, the things that "stick up" and get in the way of the Lord coming more fully into your life."

So this prophecy continues to be relevant in the present for every generation of those who follow Jesus.

As we read prophecy, we need to keep in mind that prophecies are not direct teachings. We need to understand them in their historical context, and be careful with directly and literally importing everything a prophet says to our own time. For instance, we wouldn't use the prophecy from Isaiah 40:1-3 (above) to say that God is literally going to fill up valleys and flatten mountains, and say: "This is about the invention of bulldozers!" We recognize that these are figures of speech.

Speaking of that, in any genre, it is important to distinguish a figure of speech from a literal statement. Many of the prophecies, and also the psalms, parables and proverbs, use figures of speech. So when the Bible talks about the sun running across the sky, we don't take it as a teaching that the sun has legs which it uses to run. We will consider figures of speech again in chapter 15.

THE POINT:

Prophecies are often predictions of the future, but it is not always obvious how far in the future the prophecy means. Sometimes it may have already been fulfilled. In other cases, some prophecies have yet to be fulfilled. Many Biblical prophecies were about Jesus, the Messiah, and were fulfilled in him.

Prophecy also speaks to us in our present, giving us who follow Jesus messages of hope, or correction.

14

Genre: Apocalyptic

There is a special type of prophecy called "apocalyptic." Although this type of literature is actually quite rare in the Bible, it has been very influential on American Christianity during the past 100 years or so, and mostly in ways that I believe are not legitimate. In fact, I would say that the apocalyptic parts of the Bible are by far the most misunderstood, misinterpreted, and misused parts of the Bible.

Most apocalyptic is found in parts of Ezekiel, Daniel, Zechariah and Revelation (and a few other chapters, scattered throughout some of the other prophetic books). This genre features vivid imagery, key numbers and tends to be extremely confusing. Apocalyptic often reads like someone's strange dream. Here is a relatively mild example from Zechariah:

> ₅Then the angel who talked with me came forward and said to me, "Lift your eyes and see what this is that is going out." ₆And I said, "What is it?" He said, "This is the basket that is going out." And he said, "This is their iniquity in all the land." ₇And behold, the leaden cover was lifted, and there was a woman sitting in the basket! ₈And he said, "This is Wickedness." And he thrust her back into the basket, and thrust down the leaden weight on its opening.
> ₉Then I lifted my eyes and saw, and behold, two women coming forward! The wind was in their wings. They had wings like the wings of a stork, and they lifted up the basket between earth and heaven. ₁₀Then I said to the angel who talked with me, "Where are they taking the basket?" ₁₁He said to me, "To the land of Shinar, to build a house for it. And when this is prepared, they will set the basket down there on its base." (Zech 5:5-11, ESV2011)

The apocalyptic parts of the Bible often appear to be talking about the "end times" (the period of history right before the end of the world), and they are frequently used by cults to come up with all sorts of weird doctrines.

As always, we have to read apocalyptic in context. Particularly important is to understand the historical and cultural context in which the apocalyptic prophet lived. We need to understand that the language of apocalyptic is definitely not literal, or teaching, or even narrative. It is poetic and even mystical. We need to hold firmly to the clear and easily understandable portions of the Bible, and use those to aid our understanding of apocalyptic prophecy. With apocalyptic, I am even willing to say that we should be open to the possibility that we won't completely clearly understand what is meant. We should never use apocalyptic in a way that contradicts what is already clear in different parts of the Bible.

One of the worst abuses of apocalyptic prophecy is to use it as a kind of a road-map, or detailed timeline of the end-times. It is most definitely not intended to be anything like that. Concerning the end of the world, and his return, Jesus said:

> "Now concerning that day and hour no one knows
> — neither the angels in heaven, nor the Son —
> except the Father only. (Matt 24:36, HCSB)

That is clear. Therefore, we should not interpret apocalyptic prophecy as a definitive roadmap to the end times. If it clearly gave us a timeline to the return of Jesus and the end of the old world, then Jesus would have been wrong in saying that no one can know for sure when it will be. Apocalyptic prophecy may tell us the *types* of things that will be happening, but it certainly can't be specific enough so that people will then be able to say "Aha! According to Revelation, the world will definitely end within the next three to five years!"

It is extremely important to understand that the main apocalyptic parts of the Bible were prophesied to God's people when they were severely oppressed by powerful foreign empires. Ezekiel and Daniel spoke to those who lived as captives under the Babylonians, Persians and Medes. Zechariah, not long after, prophesied to people who were trying to re-establish a colony of Jews in Israel, surrounded by powerful and lawless nations around them. John was inspired to write Revelation at a time when the Roman Emperor, Domitian, pursued the active persecution of Christians. Domitian was aided in this by some Jewish communities who saw Christianity as blasphemy, and wanted it destroyed.

Because virtually all apocalyptic prophecy was written in similar historical circumstances, there are certain features that we can learn about all of it. **Because it was written to people under foreign oppression, it contains images and pictures that would have been understandable to those for whom it was first spoken, but almost incomprehensible to outsiders.**

In other words, apocalyptic was a kind of *code language* to people in persecution.

The code is not about some secret key to the end-times – what the code hides are words of judgment upon the oppressors, and encouragement and hope for the oppressed.

The problem is that today, *we* are like the outsiders at the time it was written. In other words, the meaning of the codes is hidden from us, just as it would have been from the oppressors.

That means it is hard for us to understand the significance of the weird visions and dreams of apocalyptic literature. The first step in understanding is to realize that we do *not* understand, and we need to investigate a lot more before we can see these prophecies the same way the original hearers understood them.

Let me give you an example of "code language" from the book of Revelation. In Revelation, the number twelve is very significant. There were twelve tribes in ancient Israel. There were twelve apostles. Therefore, the number twelve is a symbol (or "code") for "the people of God." In Revelation chapter 7, it talks about 144,000 people who were sealed by God. This just means "the entire amount of God's people from both Israel and the Church." 12 tribes of Israel (representing God's people before the time of Jesus) times 12 Apostles (representing the church, God's people since the time of Jesus). 12 x 12 = 144. Get it? It isn't a literal number – it is a symbol representing "all of God's people."

You will need help to understand what the images and numbers in apocalyptic prophecy mean. And to be honest, there are still things in apocalyptic literature that no one really understands for sure. A good commentary, or study Bible, will help you understand the historical context, and give some useful suggestions about what the "code language" is really saying. However, there is a massive amount of material out there that will steer you in the wrong direction. My quick and easy way to separate a good commentary on apocalyptic from a bad, is to see if it treats apocalyptic as a timeline for the end of the world. If it does, don't bother reading it.

A study Bible will help, **but more than anything, let the clear portions of the Bible lead you in understanding what is not clear**.

Here is another thing to keep in mind: The main message of the apocalyptic prophecies is consistently one of **hope**:

God has not forgotten his people, and he will take steps to deliver them and to bring justice against those who have persecuted them. He is still active in history, he still has plans, and he intends to carry them out.

We get caught up in what, specifically, those plans are. But the main point is that God *has* them, rather than the specific details of them. Take, for example, the book of Revelation. It was written to Christians who were suffering under the oppression of the Roman government, which was aided by angry Jewish communities. When we look at the book from a big-picture perspective, we see that again and again, it repeats these messages:

- The Lord knows that you are suffering, and he hasn't forgotten you.
- Those who oppress you will be judged for what they have done.
- God has a plan to redeem and save you.
- God hasn't stopped acting in history. He has plans to bring human history to the place where he wants it to be.
- Death, and the end of history, are things for believers to look forward to – God's plans for you are wonderful, and go far beyond this life on our present earth.

These are the main things we are supposed to get from Revelation. Often we fail to get these wonderful messages of grace, because we are too caught up in things like trying to figure out which individual the anti-Christ is. But all we really need to know is that the anti-Christ is bad, and God has plans for defeating him, and protecting you from him. While he does that, you will not be forgotten, and the Lord will be with you in your trials.

Here is one more example of how to approach apocalyptic prophecy. Revelation 13:1-10 describes a "beast." Since I know the historical context of Revelation, I'm almost certain that the first readers of Revelation would have understood that the "beast" was a code word for the Roman Empire and its emperor, Domitian. Domitian demanded that everyone in the Roman world worship the Emperor as a divine being. He severely persecuted everyone who refused to do so (Jews were exempted from this, but not Christians). The first Christians to read Revelation would easily have identified what John's vision described.

But in this day and age, the same message could apply to Christians who suffer under Islamic persecution. In such places, Muslims demand that everyone must confess: "Allah is God, and Mohammed is his Prophet." Like the beast of Revelation 13, Islam has authority in many places to blaspheme (according to Christians) and to persecute those who do not agree with them or worship as Muslims.

In this way, we can see that apocalyptic prophecy can remain relevant and encouraging to Christians throughout history. My advice is to consider apocalyptic prophecy in this way, and abandon any attempts to use it as a timeline of the end times.

THE POINT:

Apocalyptic is a difficult and confusing genre. It should be treated carefully, and be sure to use the "scripture interprets scripture" rule. Let the clear parts of the Bible guide how you understand apocalyptic. This genre contains a great deal of symbolic language, "code" language, and many figures of speech. It is **not** primarily a road map of the end times, and you should avoid resources that treat it as such. The main message is one of hope for Christians who are undergoing persecution.

15

Genre: Parables, Proverbs, Poetry and Song

We will briefly consider four genres that share certain similarities. Parable, Proverb, Poetry and Song all contain imaginative and figurative language. *You might say that each of them, in different ways, conveys truth through* **word-pictures**.

Parable.

Parable is an interesting genre. Actually, it is a sort of a sub-genre of teaching. We find it mostly in the gospels, because Jesus used parables extensively. Almost always, a parable is a story that is not supposed to be taken literally, and it makes just a few main points. Don't follow rabbit trails when you deal with a parable. Stick to the main one or two points. So, consider the parable of the Good Samaritan. The main point of the story is that the Lord wants us to look after anyone in need – even our natural enemies. He wants us to treat all the people we encounter as "neighbors." The parable is not there to teach us that priests are all naturally bad people, or that we should regularly travel from Jerusalem to Jericho, or that we should pay for homeless people to stay in hotels. Stick to the main points.

Many of the parables of Jesus depend on historical and cultural knowledge that is no longer common. That means that when it comes to parables, it is often especially important to research the historical and cultural context.

Proverb.

Most of the proverbs in the Bible are contained in a book named – surprise – "Proverbs."

Proverbs, like parables, are a sub-genre of teaching. The purpose of a proverb is to teach general principles for wise living. For instance consider this one:

> 1A gentle answer turns away anger, but a harsh word stirs up wrath. (Prov 15:1, HCSB)

This is generally true. However, there are times when you might be in conflict with someone, and give that person a gentle answer, but she gets very angry anyway. Or, perhaps you say something harsh to someone, but she rises above it, and forgives you anyway. The point is not that the proverb is absolutely true, all the time. The point is that, in principle, it is usually more effective to speak gently during times of conflict. As with parables, it is possible to stretch a proverb too far. It is usually simply a wise saying, used to teach a generally wise principle.

For instance, here is another one:

> 6The house of the righteous has great wealth, but trouble accompanies the income of the wicked. (Prov 15:6, HCSB)

This saying connects wealth to the righteous, and troubled economics to the wicked. However, you cannot stretch this proverb to mean that all (or even most) righteous people are wealthy, and that those who have trouble making a living are necessarily wicked. Why not? Well, for starters, Jesus, the only person who has ever lived a truly righteous life, was not wealthy in this world. Nor were any of his apostles. Many teaching verses in the New Testament warn about earthly wealth as something that is very spiritually dangerous. For instance:

> 19"Don't collect for yourselves treasures on earth, where moth and rust destroy and where thieves break in and steal. 20But collect for yourselves treasures in heaven, where neither moth nor rust destroys, and where thieves don't break in and steal. 21For where your treasure is, there your heart will be also. (Matt 6:19-21, HCSB)

> 24"No one can be a slave of two masters, since either he will hate one and love the other, or be devoted to one and despise the other. You cannot be slaves of God and of money. (Matt 6:24, HCSB)

> 9But those who want to be rich fall into temptation, a trap, and many foolish and harmful desires, which plunge people into ruin and destruction. 10For the love of money is a root of all kinds of evil, and by craving it, some have wandered away from the faith

and pierced themselves with many pains. (1Tim 6:9-10, HCSB)

These are all from *teaching* portions of the Bible (and there are many more verses like these). Remember, we use the clear, teaching parts of the scripture to interpret parts that are less clear. Therefore, in the Proverbs verse, either "wealth" means something other than material riches, or this proverb simply cannot be stretched to make a general rule about money and righteousness.

It may surprise people to realize that Proverbs are not always true in every circumstance. This is why I am taking the time to write about them here – the genre of Proverb is not an explicit teaching, but rather, a pithy saying that captures a principle that is generally true in ordinary life. Keep in mind that there may be exceptions, and that sometimes the words are used figuratively, rather than literally.

Poetry and Song.

Many books of the Bible contain sections that were originally either songs or poetry. Because the Bible is translated from other languages, it is usually difficult to capture how it may have sounded to the original hearers. The book of Psalms is entirely made of songs and poetry. Other parts of the Bible contain poetic sections. For instance, many of the proclamations of the prophets were probably originally given in poetic language. The language of poetry and song is often not supposed to be taken literally. For example, let's look at Psalm 19.

1 The heavens declare the glory of God,
and the sky′ proclaims the work of His hands.

2 Day after day they pour out speech;
night after night they communicate knowledge.²
    3 There is no speech; there are no words;
their voice is not heard.
    4 Their message⁵ has gone out to all the earth,
and their words to the ends of the world.
In the heavens⁴ He has pitched a tent for the sun.
    5 It is like a groom coming from the⁵ bridal chamber;
it rejoices like an athlete running a course.
    6 It rises from one end of the heavens
and circles⁶ to their other end;
nothing is hidden from its heat.

First, notice that this is laid out like a poem or song. In fact, in the heading of Psalm 19, there is the note: "For the Choir Director." Most modern Bible translations will lay out poetic language in this way, even though we have no music for it, and it does not rhyme in English. This layout is the translators' way of showing us it is a song, poem or poetic prophecy. Much of Isaiah, Jeremiah and Job is laid out in this way. This lay-out is our first cue for how we should interpret the passage.

Now, in the case of Psalm 19, the writer (David) even tells us the language is poetic. In verse one, he says the heavens declare God's glory, and pour forth speech. In verse three, he clarifies that we aren't supposed to take that literally – it's a word-picture, a metaphor. He says there are no actual words, no literal voice. The sky doesn't actually talk.

In verses 4-6 David describes the sun. Now, think about the words he uses for a moment. Does this mean that the Bible teaches us that the sky is an actual covering like a tent? Do these verses teach us that the sun actually rejoices? Does it mean that no place on earth can be cold when the sun is out?

The answer to all of those questions, is, of course, no. The language is poetic. We aren't supposed to take it literally. The point is that God created the sky and all we observe in it, and by the things he set in motion in the sky, we can learn about God. This isn't a straightforward teaching. It is a song, with metaphors and similes and creative ways of expressing things. We can learn things from it (that God sends messages to us through his creation) but we get that message differently than we do when Paul says the same thing in Acts 14:15-17 and Romans 1:19-20

> What can be known about God is evident among them, because God has shown it to them. For His invisible attributes, that is, His eternal power and divine nature, have been clearly seen since the creation of the world, being understood through what He has made. As a result, people are without excuse. (Rom 1:19-20, HCSB)

This verse from Romans says basically the same thing as Psalm 19, but in a very different style. That is why genre is important for understanding. Many people make grave mistakes about the Bible when they don't consider the genre. We don't have to. It is mostly common sense, but we simply have to remember to pay attention.

THE POINT:

Parables, proverbs, poetry and songs generally teach us things through word-pictures, allegories or pithy sayings. They are not as clear as explicit teaching. Often, we are not meant to take them literally. Usually, each of these genres has one or two main points to make, and we should be careful of stretching them too far.

16

Genre: Laws

One of the most misunderstood and misused genres in the Bible is *Law*. There are three types of law in the Bible. They are as follows:

1. Civil (governmental) Law for Ancient Israel

2. Ceremonial Law about how God's people in the Old Testament were to worship and honor Him.

3. Moral Law

The first and most important purpose of all the law found in the Bible (all three types) is to show us the unfathomable distance between us and God. **In other words, the first use of the Law is to show us our sin, and our need of a savior.**

Think of it this way: in a general sense, the laws in the Bible are about God's objective, unchanging standard of holiness. God is holy – that is his nature. God's holiness is, in effect, one of the basic laws of the universe, like the law of gravity, or the laws concerning the properties of light or matter. God's holiness is so powerful that it destroys all unholiness. Therefore, if you are unholy and you come into the presence of God, you will be destroyed.

The "law" is simply a way for us to measure our holiness, to see if we can come into God's presence or not. It tells us if we are holy or not. If we are not holy, God cannot approve of us. Instead, his nature destroys us.

Picture a high jump – two upright poles with a crosspiece between them. The idea is, you have to jump over the crosspiece without knocking it down. The world record high jump is 2.45 meters, or about 8 feet. Now imagine a high jump with the crossbar set at sixteen feet, or five meters – twice as high as the highest any human has ever jumped. The bar up there shows you exactly how high you need to jump. There is nothing wrong with the measurement. The measurement is accurate and correct. It is good. It would be terrific to jump that high.

But the measurement simply shows you what you must do. It does not help you to do it. It cannot help you – that's not what a measurement is for. So if the measurement shows you that you fall short, that's not the fault of the measurement. It doesn't mean the measurement is wrong or bad. It just shows you that you failed to reach the standard. The problem is not with the measurement, it is with *you*.

The law simply shows us what holiness looks like. It provides a way for us to measure and see if we have reached it or not. The standard is what it is, because holiness is what it is. It is a law of God's nature. **And what the law shows us is that we cannot reach the standard**. We cannot be holy enough to be justified, to be proven right in God's eyes. The law shows us that the standard is impossible. That is all that the law can accomplish. It shows us that we are not holy, that we are sinners. And every time you try and reach that standard, the law will show you the same thing again. Because of the sin of Adam and Eve, we were born without a chance. We were born with a congenital illness called sin, and the law shows us that we simply cannot overcome that. **The law is not a means to get right with God. It is a measurement that shows that on our own, we can *never* get right with God**.

Now, if we cannot get right with God, what hope do we have? Only this: justification through Jesus Christ. "Justification" is the process by which we are made holy, so that we can experience the presence of God. It doesn't come through the law. It comes through Jesus. In and through Jesus Christ, all the righteous demands of the law – of God's holiness – were fulfilled – *on our behalf*. He suffered and died – as punishment for *our failure* to meet the holiness standard. He rose again and imparts eternal "resurrection-life" to us. **All that is left for us to do is to trust that this is indeed true**. Jesus said:

> 17"Don't assume that I came to destroy the Law or the Prophets. I did not come to destroy but to fulfill.
> 18For I assure you: Until heaven and earth pass away, not the smallest letter or one stroke of a letter

will pass from the law until all things are
accomplished. (Matt 5:17-18, HCSB)

Jesus accomplished the law himself, on our behalf. Paul
explains it like this:

21But now, apart from the law, God's righteousness
has been revealed — attested by the Law and the
Prophets 22— that is, God's righteousness through
faith in Jesus Christ, to all who believe, since there
is no distinction. 23For all have sinned and fall short
of the glory of God. 24They are justified freely by His
grace through the redemption that is in Christ
Jesus. 25God presented Him as a propitiation
through faith in His blood, to demonstrate His
righteousness, because in His restraint God passed
over the sins previously committed. 26God
presented Him to demonstrate His righteousness at
the present time, so that He would be righteous and
declare righteous the one who has faith in Jesus.
(Rom 3:21-26, HCSB)

So the first purpose, or use, of any law in the Bible is to
expose our own un-holiness. It shows us our desperate need
for God to act somehow on our behalf. **The law shows us our
sin, our need for Jesus Christ, and encourages us to
receive what he has done for us**.

Now, does this mean that once we trust Jesus there is no
need to pay attention any more to the laws in the Bible?

Not at all. It is true, however, that many Christians are
confused about this. To better grasp the way those who are
saved by Jesus should interpret laws, let's look at each of the
three types, one by one.

1. LAWS OF ANCIENT ISRAEL

The laws for ancient Israel are exactly that: laws that applied literally and directly to the nation of Israel from about 1400 BC until Jerusalem was destroyed in 587 BC. No one lives in ancient Israel any more – that nation has not existed for more than 2,000 years. Today, there is a modern nation of Israel, but it is set up with a constitution and a set of laws that are different from those given by Moses. But long before that, even by the time of Jesus, the ancient nation of Israel had ceased to exist. So, when we read a law that applies to citizenship in ancient Israel, we know right away that we should not apply it *literally*, without further investigation.

Some Jewish leaders once tried to trick Jesus with one of these ancient laws. They caught a woman in adultery, and brought her to him, and said "According to the Law, we should stone her." They were referring to Leviticus 20:10,

> 10If a man commits adultery with a married woman
> — if he commits adultery with his neighbor's wife
> — both the adulterer and the adulteress must be put to death. (Lev 20:10, HCSB)

The truth was, they weren't serious. At the time of Jesus, the Jews lived under Roman law, which forbade such things. It was illegal for them to stone her. If Jesus affirmed the Old Testament law, they could bring him before the Romans for attempted murder. If Jesus rejected the law, they could claim to his followers that he did not follow the teaching of Moses. It's the same thing I've seen countless times on blogs and social media posts: "You claim to follow the Bible, but the Bible says *this*. Are you going to do that, or not?"

Jesus knew it was a trap. He couldn't explain about ancient laws without being misquoted. So he said

> "The one without sin among you should be the first
> to throw a stone at her." (John 8:7, HCSB)

Caught in their own trap, they left. When they were gone, he told the woman that he did not condemn her (meaning, condemn her to death, *according to the laws of ancient Israel*) but he also said: "Go, and from now on, do not sin anymore." (John 8:11). The whole story is in John 8:1-11. It shows us Jesus' attitude toward two kinds of laws. The laws of the ancient nation of Israel no longer apply in the literal sense. Jesus himself changed all that (more on that in the next paragraph). But the moral law – "do not commit adultery" – still applies. Jesus called it a sin, and told the woman to stop it.

There is something else. The law of death for adulterers *was* fulfilled. There *was* death for the woman who committed adultery, the one they brought to Jesus. Only, it wasn't *her* death. Jesus died in her place. **He did not set aside the law – he fulfilled it**. Death came as a result of her sin. This is why she did not have to be condemned – he chose to fulfill the law on her behalf. He also chose to fulfill the law on *our* behalf. Do you see, how (as Jesus said) all the law and the prophets are fulfilled in Jesus? When we understand that, so much more of the Bible opens up for us.

Even though the ancient laws of the Israelite nation no longer apply in a direct, literal sense, they do still apply in the sense that they teach us important eternal principles. We no longer directly apply the law "death to adulterers." But it still *means* something for us. It means that adultery is a very serious thing in God's eyes. It is a graphic illustration, even today, that sin leads to death. It shows us again our need for Jesus, and how amazing is his love and grace to us.

So these ancient civil laws are fulfilled in the life, death and resurrection of Jesus. What remains are not things for us to do, but principles that we can learn. Paul demonstrated this when he referred to the law about not muzzling oxen (1 Corinthians 9, mentioned in chapter 6 of this book). That is no longer a law for anyone to obey literally. It was given as a civil law for ancient Israel, which, again, has not existed for 2,500 years. But that ancient law does contain an eternal principle that we should try to apply to our own lives as Jesus-followers. The same is true of all of those ancient-Israel laws. Sometimes it takes work to uncover the principle. We have to read in context, and learn the cultural and historical setting of those laws. We are guided by the New Testament. We don't apply these things directly and literally. But there is good stuff for us there.

2. LAWS REGARDING WORSHIP CEREMONIES

There are hundreds of laws in the Old Testament about how the people of Israel were to worship God. Among these are laws about what makes a person ceremonially "clean" or "unclean," and what we call "kosher" laws about food. Thankfully, the New Testament is very clear about all of this. Jesus himself said:

> "Are you also as lacking in understanding? Don't you realize that nothing going into a man from the

> outside can defile him? For it doesn't go into his heart but into the stomach and is eliminated." (As a result, He made all foods clean.) Then He said, "What comes out of a person — that defiles him. For from within, out of people's hearts, come evil thoughts, sexual immoralities, thefts, murders, adulteries, greed, evil actions, deceit, promiscuity, stinginess, blasphemy, pride, and foolishness. All these evil things come from within and defile a person." (Mark 7:18-23, HCSB)

Mark comments "As a result, He made all foods clean." He is clear that Jesus eliminated the kosher laws, while, at the same time, affirming the moral laws.

Peter had a vision that confirmed the fact that kosher laws are not necessary for those who are in Jesus (Acts 10:9-16). The first apostles wrestled with what the ceremonial laws meant after Jesus' life, death and resurrection. Acts 15:28-29 records their conclusions:

> For it has seemed good to the Holy Spirit and to us to lay on you no greater burden than these requirements: that you abstain from idol-offerings, and from blood, from smothering [abortion], and from sexual immorality. If you keep yourselves from these, you will do well. Farewell." (Acts 15:28-29 My rendering from Greek. The word variously translated "what is strangled" or "smothered" was a colloquial expression referring to the practice of smothering unwanted newborn infants)

In other words, the New Testament permits you to eat all the bacon-wrapped shrimp that you want; while affirming, like Jesus did, that believers in Jesus should continue to try to follow the *moral* law. More on that in the next section.

In addition, the book of Hebrews deals extensively with the laws regarding worship. The short version is this: All of the Old Testament worship ceremonies and practices were designed to do two things: 1. Show us our need for a Messiah/Savior and 2. Help us to understand what he would do for us.

Therefore, Jesus fulfilled all of these laws. It is not necessary for us to practice them anymore.

> These serve as a copy and shadow of the heavenly things, as Moses was warned when he was about to complete the tabernacle. For God said, **Be careful that you make everything according to the pattern that was shown to you on the mountain.** But Jesus has now obtained a superior ministry, and to that degree He is the mediator of a better covenant, which has been legally enacted on better promises. (Heb 8:5-6, HCSB)

> Since the law has only a shadow of the good things to come, and not the actual form of those realities, it can never perfect the worshipers by the same sacrifices they continually offer year after year. (Heb 10:1, HCSB)

So we do not need to sacrifice animals in worship, or wear special clothes, or burn incense, or live "kosher" or follow any of those Old Testament regulations for worship or festivals and feasts. Those laws were all only a shadow of the reality that was fulfilled in Jesus Christ.

However, learning about those things can still greatly enrich our appreciation and understanding of Jesus and what he has done for us. For example, our family has celebrated the Passover Feast for the past 20 years. We don't believe it is necessary. But it is a helpful tradition that points us toward Jesus and reminds us of all the promises God fulfilled in Him. We can learn similar things by studying other Old Testament worship laws. But we do not have to literally follow them as written.

3. MORAL LAWS

The moral laws in the Bible are a reflection of God's Holy nature. In a sense *all* laws are moral laws, in that they express something about God's holy nature. But what we generally call "the moral laws" are *direct* expressions of what God considers right and wrong, and they are usually not connected to any particular culture, government or style of worship. For example: "Do not murder" (Exodus 20:13) is a moral law. It is a direct expression of right and wrong.

Moral laws do not change. The Ten Commandments are moral laws. Laws about not hating and sexual purity and loving others are all moral laws. Usually you can identify moral laws because they are very direct, and they are not connected to civil government or worship ceremonies.

The New Testament teaches that Jesus fulfilled the entire moral law for us, so we do not have to do the impossible task of keeping the moral law perfectly. However, Jesus, living inside us, wants to continue to keep the moral law. He doesn't want to hate, or murder, or commit sexual sin or lie or cheat. **Therefore the moral law remains a standard for Christians**. Jesus himself affirmed the Ten Commandments. He affirmed that sexual purity is found in abstinence before marriage, and faithfulness in marriage. He affirmed that we should love others, and not hate. He taught that lies and oppression were sinful. The apostles of Jesus also affirmed the moral law in every book of the New Testament.

Thanks to Jesus, the moral law is no longer a standard we must reach *in order to be reconciled to God*. Jesus has already done that for us. Even so, it is good to want to please God by doing the right thing. I'm pleased when I see my kids following the moral law - being kind, being responsible, staying away from drugs and so on. But it doesn't cause me to love them more nor does it have any bearing upon their identity as my kids.

We can't keep it perfectly, but when we break the moral law, it is a sign that there is something wrong in our relationship with Jesus. We are not meant to engage in a lifestyle in which we regularly break the moral law that is a reflection of the Holy nature of God. When we do as we please, and consistently, deliberately live in a pattern of breaking the moral law, we reveal that either we don't have real faith in Jesus, or that we are in danger of rejecting Jesus.

It is like a warning sign. The moral law tells us when we are in danger of messing up our lives. It tells us when we are in danger of moving away from Jesus, and heading toward rejecting who He is, and what he has done for us. It is a message that shouts "Danger! Wrong Way! Turn Back! Death Ahead!" We ignore the moral law to our own peril and destruction.

I encourage you to take some time with this chapter. As you do, I encourage you to listen to the Holy Spirit. This is an important subject that too few Christians genuinely understand.

THE POINT:

First and foremost, the law shows us our own sin, our own failure and inability to meet God's holy standard. It drives us to despair of our own efforts and to trust instead the efforts of Jesus on our behalf.

Once we trust Jesus and begin to walk with him, we do not need to be afraid of the law any more. In Jesus, the law is no longer dangerous and condemning – it is a blessing. The ancient laws of Israel show us eternal principles that should still be applied today, though the applications may look very different than they did in ancient times. The ceremonial laws also teach us eternal truths, and show us God's holiness, and remind us how much we need Jesus, and how Jesus fulfilled the holy standard of the law on our behalf. The moral laws protect us, by keeping us away from danger, and close to God.

PART III: ADDITIONAL QUESTIONS

17

What did Jesus Say?

Recently, someone showed me a post on Facebook. The caption said: "What Jesus said about Homosexuality." Underneath it was...nothing. That's accurate, in a technical sense, but it is not the complete story. For one thing, Jesus' apostles did say some things about the subject, elsewhere in the New Testament. In any case, the point, presumably, is that Christians should not be saying anything about it, since Jesus didn't. A similar issue was raised by an Albanian man that I spoke with in Corfu, Greece, one time when I was on a mission trip. He argued that Jesus never claimed to be God –

instead, that claim was made by the apostles, not Jesus himself.

Both of these arguments depend upon the same kind of faulty reasoning, and the same silly and inconsistent approach to the Bible. **The first part of it** goes like this: "It's supposed to be all about Jesus, right? So I'll listen only to the words of Jesus. What the apostles wrote doesn't matter."

Let's look at this by using another issue, one that is not controversial today. Here it is, another thing that is technically true: **Jesus never said anything about slavery**. Think about that for a moment. What does that mean? Did Jesus endorse slavery? Does that mean we Christians should not call slave-trading wrong and sinful?

Now, class it's time to see if you've been paying attention. Does anyone remember where the New Testament came from? How is it that we know what Jesus said in the first place? *The apostles heard it, taught it, and wrote it down.* To put it another way, it is the *apostles* who gave us the words of Jesus. If you don't want to pay attention to what the apostles wrote, than you cannot pay attention to what Jesus said either, since we got *that* also from the apostles.

Let's look at it another way. In chapter four, we examined a lot of evidence suggesting that the apostles wrote reliably and accurately about real historical events and situations, and also about Jesus and his teaching. There is no legitimate reason to accept the gospels, *which were written by his apostles*, but not the other writings of the other apostles. If you believe that the apostles correctly recorded that Jesus said, "Love your neighbor," you have exactly the same reasons for believing that the apostles are passing on the teaching of Jesus when they tell us that slave-trading is evil (1 Timothy 1:10) – even though we cannot find Jesus directly saying so in the gospels.

To put it simply: the **entire New Testament** *is the teaching of, and about Jesus*. It all comes from the same source – the Holy Spirit, who inspired the apostles to remember and write. We know what Jesus said, because the apostles wrote it down. Although the letters of the New Testament are in a different *form* than the gospels, they are still the teachings of Jesus, passed on by the apostles. In other words, what Paul writes in Romans should be just as important to us as what Jesus says in the book of Mark.

There's another thing. John makes it clear that his own gospel does not contain every single word that Jesus ever said. The way he puts it, not even the other three gospels would suffice to contain everything Jesus did and said:

> And there are also many other things that Jesus did, which, if they were written one by one, I suppose not even the world itself could contain the books that would be written. (John 21:25, HCSB)

Jesus told the apostles that the Holy Spirit would remind them of what he said, and make it clear to them, and *also tell them other things that they need to know*:

> "I still have many things to tell you, but you can't bear them now. When the Spirit of truth comes, He will guide you into all the truth. For He will not speak on His own, but He will speak whatever He hears. He will also declare to you what is to come. He will glorify Me, because He will take from what is Mine and declare it to you. Everything the Father has is Mine. This is why I told you that He takes

from what is Mine and will declare it to you. (John
16:12-15, HCSB)

We believe, as Jesus said, that the Holy Spirit reminded
the apostles what Jesus said, and also revealed other
important truths to them, and guided them as they wrote it
down. That applies, not just to the gospels, but to the entire
New Testament. In this passage, Jesus himself says that after
he leaves this world, the Spirit would guide them into truth
that they had not yet received from him. So, if you don't
believe the Holy Spirit inspired Paul to write what Jesus
thinks about slave-trading, why do you believe he inspired
Luke to write that Jesus has concern for the poor?

Therefore, the first answer to the person who claims that
Jesus said nothing about a given topic, is to see whether that
topic shows up anywhere else in the New Testament. If it
does, than you can be sure, it **is** the teaching of Jesus.
Technically, it's true that Matthew, Mark, Luke and John do
not record any direct quotes of Jesus that use the word "slave-
trader." But Paul, inspired by the Holy Spirit to share the
teaching of, and about, Jesus, *does* say something about it.

Some people will argue that Paul did not know Jesus
personally, and so his letters are not the real teaching of
Jesus. We went over that in chapter four. Paul claimed that
Jesus appeared to him specially, quite some time after his
resurrection, and opened his mind to know and understand
the Good News (Galatians 2:1-16; 1 Corinthians 15:8-10; 2
Corinthians 12:1-7). The other apostles, the ones who had
actually known Jesus, affirmed that Paul was preaching and
teaching the true message of Jesus (Galatian 2:6-10; 2 Peter

153

3:15-16; Acts 9:22-30; 15:1-35). In fact, all throughout the book of Acts, we have ample evidence that Paul was accepted early on as an apostle of Jesus, and his teaching was in accord with the rest of the apostles.

Let me say it again: **the entire New Testament, *including the letters of Paul*, is the teaching of Jesus**, passed on by the Holy Spirit, through the apostles. We have all sorts of evidence to affirm this, and none to contradict it.

Saying "I only believe or follow the words in red [Jesus' words]," is in fact, silly and illogical. The "words in red" came from the same place as the rest of the New Testament – the apostles. If you don't believe the apostles were inspired by the Holy Spirit and the memory of Jesus' teachings to write what they wrote in their letters, there is no reason to believe that they got the words of Jesus in the gospels correct either.

I want to explore one more side of the "Jesus didn't say anything about this" issue. Recently, in a small group meeting, I pointed out that Jesus never said anything about slavery. One of the excellent teenagers who was present said, "Yeah, but doesn't the golden rule kind of cover that?" In other words, though he didn't specifically talk about slavery, Jesus *did* say, "Do unto others as you would have them do unto you." In this way, according to the teaching of Jesus, if you don't think you'd like being a slave yourself, you shouldn't make slaves of anyone else.

This is a great point. Jesus did not overtly condemn prostitution, child-pornography, or incest, either. But you don't have to be a trained theologian to recognize that Jesus often said things that apply to a whole host of different situations. In Matthew 19:1-6. Jesus made a broad, sweeping statement about human sexual relationships. He said that God created sex for marriage between a man and a woman. Any kind of sex outside of the marriage relationship is called, in Greek, "porneia." The most popular English bibles translate this "sexual immorality," or "immorality." Jesus didn't name all the possibilities included in "sexual immorality," but he made it clear that he meant anything sexual outside of one-woman/one man marriage. In Matthew 15:19, among other places, he makes it clear that all sexual immorality creates a problem with God's moral law.

The point is not to condemn anyone who has sinned in this way. Jesus has fulfilled the moral law on our behalf, and if we trust him, we are forgiven, though Christians should not continue to engage in sexual immorality. The point is, Jesus did in fact teach about all human sexuality, even if he didn't specifically name certain sins. If we claim to follow him, we should at least be heading in the direction he points, even if we follow imperfectly.

This turns out be the case concerning most of the other things that Jesus did not specifically talk about. And, as we have said, even when Jesus didn't say something specifically in one of the gospels, we have the rest of the New Testament which also reliably passes on the teaching of, and about, Jesus.

THE POINT:

Christians believe the **entire Bible** is the inspired Word of God. This means that the same Holy Spirit who inspired the

155

apostles to remember what Jesus said and did, also inspired every other part of the Bible. All of it is God's word to us. Singling out the words of Jesus as somehow "more authoritative" has never been a legitimate Christian practice, and besides, it is illogical, since Jesus himself did not physically write any part of the Bible.

18

Versions and Verses

I want to consider which Bible versions are most helpful to use, and why.

Obviously, any Bible that is in any language other than Hebrew, Aramaic and Greek is a translation. One thing we should keep in mind about translation is that it is almost impossible to translate something word-for-word from one language into another.

Let's look at one of my favorite Bible verses as an example:

> We know that all things work together for the good of those who love God: those who are called according to His purpose. (Rom 8:28, HCSB)

Let me give this to you in the most literal way possible from the Greek:

> "Know-we and that to-the-ones loving The God all
> works-together for good, to-the-ones according-to
> purpose called being."

Where I have linked English words with a dash, there is
only one Greek word that encompasses the same meaning as
the two or more English words do when joined together. You
can see that a word for word literal translation is impossible.
In Greek "We know" is all one word. "To-the-ones" is all one
word. In addition, grammar and the placement of verbs is
different from Greek to English.

Keeping this in mind, there are two general approaches to
Bible translation. The first, more scholarly approach, is called
"Formal Equivalence." In this approach, translators try to
create a version that is as *close* to word-for-word as possible,
though of course *true* word-for-word is impossible. The
advantage of this is that the resulting translation gives you a
better idea of how it was actually written. The downside is
that this often makes for complicated and confusing English
grammar. A good example of formal equivalence is the *New
American Standard Bible* (NASB).

The other approach is called "Functional Equivalence." In
this approach, translators focus on the meaning of the text,
and then seek to express that meaning in clear, readable
language. The positive of this approach is that it makes the
Bible easier to understand. The negative is that sometimes
the translators are actually *interpreting* the Bible for readers
and coming up with a meaning that might not have been
originally intended. They might also miss a double-meaning
that was intended by the original language.

For instance, the New International Version (NIV) consistently translates the Greek word "*sarx*" as "sinful nature." However, the word actually means "flesh." The New Testament does use this word, *flesh*, as a description of the part of us that is prone to corruption and sin. Paul says, "I know that nothing good lives in me, that is my flesh." (Romans 7:18). But it is an *interpretation*, not just a *translation*, to make *sarx* "sinful nature." If you don't know Greek, the NIV has already decided for you how you should understand the word. Personally, I feel that "sinful nature" is a misleading term, and does not fully capture what the New Testament means by *sarx* (flesh).

Most English Bible translations fall somewhere in between formal equivalence and functional equivalence, though usually they tend more towards one or the other.

There is a third approach, represented by English versions of the Bible that go even beyond functional equivalence. These are not translations at all, but rather, *paraphrases*. The editor, or editors, of paraphrased bibles decide what the verses mean, and then put that meaning into their own words in a way that they think is relevant and helpful. These days, one of the most popular paraphrase Bibles is *The Message*. The great advantage of a paraphrase is that the meanings of verses are expressed very clearly and understandably. The disadvantage is that you are relying on someone else (the editor) to tell you not just what it says, but also what it *means*, and that person may get it wrong. *The Message* can be very helpful in making you look at verses in a new way. However, the entire thing is the work of just one person, and, as such, at times, it will inevitably reflect his own biases and failings.

I myself favor translations that lean towards formal equivalence, but also do a good job of making things clear and readable. I think the two best overall versions in terms of both accuracy and readability are the *Holman Christian Standard Bible* (HCSB) and the *English Standard Version* (ESV). I slightly favor the HCSB, but I use both regularly.

If you are wondering about the King James Version (KJV) of the Bible, and why I haven't mentioned it here, please see Appendix B.

What about the Verses and Chapters in the Bible?

Throughout this book, I use references like this: John "3:16." "John," of course, represents the book of John. "3" means I am talking about chapter three. "16" shows you that I am talking about verse sixteen.

Though the titles of the books appear in the original Greek and Hebrew, the chapter and verse markings in modern Bibles are not part of the original texts. Over the years, different scholars and church leaders added chapter and verse divisions to make it easier to describe and find various parts of scripture. The chapters and verses most bibles use today were put into place around 1650 AD.

There is one other thing that might be helpful to know. In most of the ancient Greek texts, there is no punctuation, and no indication of paragraphs. Bible translators are skilled experts, and in general, we can rely on the punctuation and paragraphs that they use. However, at times, you may find yourself thinking something like: "This sentence or verse seems like it goes better with the preceding paragraph or chapter than the one it is attached to." At times, you could be right about that, since translators often have to make a judgement call. Again, however, most respectable Bible translation projects employ scholars who have spent a lifetime immersed in Greek or Hebrew, and so in general, you should acknowledge that they are likely to know better than you.

The point is, use the chapter and verse markings to find things, and to communicate to others which parts of the Bible you are talking about, but do not rely on them to determine meaning.

THE POINT:

To really understand the Bible, I recommend mainly using a translation made using the formal equivalence approach. As of this writing, the ESV (English Standard Version) and HCSB (Holman Christian Standard Bible) are excellent versions. Use paraphrases like *The Message* sparingly, almost as a commentary, after you have already read the passage in a formal equivalence translation.

19

Practical Tools

I want to offer you some practical advice that will help you understand and study the Bible for yourself.

First, to really get a grasp on things, you need the right tools. Though a lot of the Bible is easy to understand, Bible study is, in fact, an ancient and scholarly discipline. You don't need an advanced degree to get a lot out of the Bible, but it really is worth a little time and effort on your part to understand it better. In other words, if you are going to look at the Bible as a primary source of wisdom and guidance for your life (and I highly recommend that you do) you should take it seriously.

Start with a high-quality, understandable modern-English translation.

As I mentioned in the last chapter, I highly recommend the English Standard Version (ESV) and also the Holman Christian Standard Bible (HCSB). Both of them are highly accurate compared with the original Greek and Hebrew. The ESV renders the Greek and Hebrew a little more literally – as much like "word for word" as possible. The HCSB is also very accurate, but is willing to "bend" a little to make it more readable.

One of the most popular translations is the New International Version (NIV) but, for a variety of reasons, I have lost confidence in the newer editions of that version.

I realize that *The Message* is very easy to understand, and is tremendously popular, but it is a paraphrase, and it has significant drawbacks. In my opinion, *The Message* really shines when rendering Paul's letters, but often misses the boat when it comes to the Gospels. In any case, it simply isn't good to rely mainly on *The Message*.

You can buy both the ESV and the HCSB online, or at many local bookstores or bookstore chains. You can also get them free with various Bible apps or software programs. I highly recommend getting a *study Bible* version of one of these translations. A study Bible is a Bible that has notes (usually on the lower half of the page) giving background and explanation about the verses you are reading. Study bibles are a very helpful tool when you are just getting started, and even as you learn more.

I have an inexpensive Android tablet, and on it, I use the free Olive Tree Bible Study app. Look it up in Google Play, or from your apple device. The link here will take you to their free Bible translations page, which includes my two favorite translations, the ESV and the HCSB. I paid extra to get the ESV Study Bible notes, to attach to whatever translation I'm reading in the app.

I also found a great free web-based study Bible, built on the HCSB, at https://www.mywsb.com/.

You may wonder how to learn the cultural and historical background that is so important for understanding the Bible. Certainly, my own blog (found at www.revth.wordpress.com), and other sound preachers and teachers are a good place to start. I also recently found Fred Wright's Manners and Customs of Bible Times as a free PDF download. It's a great historical/cultural resource. It was written in 1953, but all Bible-times were before that, so it's still accurate!

I also highly recommend *Eerdmans' Handbook to the Bible*. I own the British version of this, which was given to me by my parents when I was thirteen years old. The information I learned from it is still helpful to me today, and I still occasionally use it as a reference. *Zondervan's Handbook to the Bible* is the latest version of that, but I have not personally looked at it to see what they might have changed.

Another very helpful tool in this day and age is a good computer program for Bible Study. Over the years, I have paid hundreds of dollars for various versions of three different programs (*QuickVerse*, *PC Study Bible* and *Logos*). However, a few years ago I settled on a fourth, *free* program that is truly excellent: The Word (www.theword.net). If you do end up using and appreciating The Word, I encourage you to donate something to the program's creator, Konstantinos Stergiou –

I did (and I get nothing from this – I just think the guy deserves to be blessed for his amazing work, offered for free). The program may take a little while to learn, but it's worth it, and there are a number of free tutorials. There are hundreds of free add-on resources you can use with *The Word* to enhance your Bible Study, and there are paid modules as well, if you are interested.

If you are staying "old school" and prefer physical books, I do recommend that you get a Bible that includes both cross references, and a concordance in the back. I covered cross-references in chapter nine. You can learn a lot by following the cross references to other parts of the Bible. This helps the Bible to "explain itself," so to speak. A concordance is a list of words that appear in the Bible, and where. There are some stand-alone exhaustive concordances, but most study bibles have decent partial-concordances in the back. They are helpful for finding verses if you only remember a key word, or for helping you understand how certain words are used throughout scripture.

Revisit this book from time to time – we've covered a lot of ground that should help you understand the Bible better as you encounter parts of it that seem difficult.

~

All right, let's say you have assembled your tools. You have a book on the historical and cultural background of the Bible. You have a study Bible, or Bible app, with the ability to find cross references and search for specific words. Maybe you have a computer program, or a web-based Bible-software program. Now what?

First, because context is so important, read through one book of the Bible at a time, however slowly. Say you decide to read through Matthew. Before you start, read the introduction in your study Bible. Look up Matthew in *Eerdman's Handbook to the Bible*. Now, pray for God to speak to you through the Bible. The Bible describes itself as God's revelation to human beings. We cannot receive it or understand it without his help, so ask for that help. Next, read the first chapter of Matthew. The first seventeen verses of it is *genealogy*, so use your cross references, concordance, or your computer Bible program to look up some of the people listed there. Record your thoughts, discoveries, and insights in a journal, or on your computer. Probably that is plenty for one session.

The next time you read, pray once more for the Holy Spirit to teach you, and then start where you left off, say, at Matthew 1:18, and finish the chapter. Look up ancient Jewish marriage traditions in Manners and Customs of Bible Times. Read the study-Bible commentary if you feel the need to. Write down your discoveries and insights. Don't forget to write down questions also. Ask God about the questions you have, and investigate them. Often, the richest times of spiritual discovery through the Bible come from our difficult questions.

It is normal to have some days where you read your next portion of scripture, and you have no particularly helpful thoughts or insights. Don't worry when that happens. I generally eat three meals a day. I couldn't tell you what I had for dinner a week ago – it wasn't that memorable. But it nourished my body, just the same. **In the same way, the Bible will nourish your spirit, even when you don't realize it is happening**.

Continue on this way until you finish the whole book of Matthew. It may take you a month, or six months. You don't get a gold star for *finishing* – the point is to immerse yourself in the Bible on a regular basis, so there's no advantage to hurrying. When you finish Matthew, pick another book of the Bible, and go through the same process.

I think this is the best way to get the most out of the Bible over a lifetime. It isn't the only way, however. Let me suggest another way, perhaps more simple, to find insights from the Bible.

First, keep in mind all you have learned in this book. As always, read any passage of scripture in context: what does it say before and after the part you are reading? Again, because context is so important, I encourage you to work your way through entire books of the Bible, however slowly, rather than jumping around. Learn about the history and culture, as necessary. Pay attention to the genre. Check cross references. Remember to use the clear parts of the Bible to help you understand what is not clear, and consider ways to harmonize apparent contradictions. Look up key words in a dictionary and concordance. Remember, especially, that the purpose of the whole Bible is to reveal Jesus Christ to us.

And then do this: SPECK. Look at the passage you want to study, and go through SPECK, one letter at a time.

S – Read the verses and see if there is a *sin* identified here. Is the Lord calling you to repent of it? Is he warning you to stay away from it?

P – Read the verses again, this time looking for *promises*. Is the Lord speaking to you through a promise here? If you are ambitious, you can also look for *prophecies* (which also begin with "p").

E – Read the verses yet again, now looking for *encouragement* and *exhortation*. How does the Lord want to cheer you on through these verses? How is he calling you to keep going?

C – Now read through your passage and see if there are any *commands* to consider. Is the Lord asking you to respond to him in a certain way through these verses?

K – read a fifth time. Is there any information or *knowledge* that you have gained from these verses?

After you SPECK, I encourage you to write a short note/prayer to the Lord. Something simple like this:

Lord, as I read John 3:16-18, I see that sometimes I sin by not trusting you. But I also hear your promise that as I trust you, you save me. You don't condemn me. Thank you for your mercy and grace! Increase my trust in you! Help me to trust you in these things that are going on in my life right now, as well as for eternal life. AMEN

Writing down your thoughts or prayers helps to solidify God's word to you in your mind and heart. If you do it regularly over time, later it becomes a source of encouragement and hope to go back and see how God has spoken to you throughout the years.

I hope and pray that you have been encouraged to learn that the Bible is a unique and amazing book. I hope and pray that you will devote time and energy to reading it and understanding it.

20

Difficult Passages

Hopefully, you have already begun to develop a solid foundation for how to understand the Bible. In this chapter, I will give you an example of how to apply the tools we have learned so far, to a difficult passage of the Bible.

Let's consider one of those Bible passages that I call "annihilation clauses."

> 16However, you must not let any living thing survive among the cities of these people the LORD your God is giving you as an inheritance. 17You must completely destroy them — the Hittite, Amorite, Canaanite, Perizzite, Hivite, and Jebusite — as the LORD your God has commanded you, 18so that they won't teach you to do all the detestable things they do for their gods, and you sin against the LORD your God. (Deut 20:16-18, HCSB)

This passage commands the people of Israel to utterly destroy, not just enemy warriors, but every living thing. That includes women, children and even livestock.

This seems monstrous to most modern readers. Why would God command his people to be so utterly brutal? Also, these types of verses often raise other questions, like: What does this mean for us today? Is Holy War acceptable? What possible value can we find in these scriptures?

Let's begin by doing the work we now understand that we should do when interpreting the Bible. **We start with context, both textual and historical**.

First, do the verses themselves contain any reason for this difficult command? In fact, they do. Verse 18 tells us that the reason for this is so that the tribes of Canaan do not lead the people of Israel away from the Lord.

Continuing with context, if we have been reading through the whole book of Deuteronomy, and if we have done our homework as outlined in this book, we will know that Deuteronomy is the record of Moses' last words, given before he died, and before the people entered the Promised Land. The entire book contains a great deal of instruction for how the people of Israel are to deal with the tribes they find in the promised land, and how they are to organize their own new nation. Chapter twenty is basically dedicated to the topic of warfare with the tribes of Canaan. Just prior to these verses, it gives instructions for making war with nations and tribes who are not in the Promised Land itself. Next, the topic turns to war with the tribes that actually live in the land that the

Lord is giving to Israel. It is in this context that we read God's command through Moses.

Understanding the context, **we continue by observing the genre**. We see that this is a law given to the ancient nation of Israel. Immediately then, we understand that this law no longer applies in a literal sense to anyone living today. It is a law for ancient Israel, a nation which no longer exists. Therefore, we cannot use this as some sort of justification for killing anyone we think is an enemy of God. Neither can we use it as justification for killing all enemies of the country we live in, since we don't live in ancient Israel. We cannot apply these verses directly and literally to our own situation.

I have already argued, however, that the entire Bible is still useful to followers of Jesus Christ. So we are still left with the question: What use can we get out of these verses?

Let's investigate further by looking up some cross references.

One is Leviticus 18:21-30, where the Lord describes some of the vile practices of the Canaanites.

> 21 "You are not to make any of your children pass through the fire to Molech. Do not profane the name of your God; I am Yahweh. 22 You are not to sleep with a man as with a woman; it is detestable. 23 You are not to have sexual intercourse with any animal, defiling yourself with it; a woman is not to present herself to an animal to mate with it; it is a perversion.
> 24 "Do not defile yourselves by any of these practices, **for the nations I am driving out before you have defiled themselves by all these things.** 25 The land has become defiled, so I am punishing it

for its sin, and the land will vomit out its inhabitants.

26But you are to keep My statutes and ordinances. You must not commit any of these detestable things — not the native or the foreigner who lives among you. 27For the men who were in the land prior to you have committed all these detestable things, and the land has become defiled. 28If you defile the land, it will vomit you out as it has vomited out the nations that were before you.

29Any person who does any of these detestable practices must be cut off from his people. 30You must keep My instruction to not do any of the detestable customs that were practiced before you, so that you do not defile yourselves by them; I am Yahweh your God." (Lev 18:21-30, HCSB, emphasis mine)

The Canaanite tribes engaged in ritual prostitution. They sacrificed their children to false gods in acts of demonic worship, burning the infants alive. They accepted sexual perversions, including sex with animals. Their religion and culture was like a cancer. It was a cancer situated in a prime spot to spread quickly around the entire world, as subsequent history proved. So God had to take the extreme measure of completely removing the cancer before it metastasized. He did not want traders and travelers carrying these depraved and demonic ideas around the world.

Another cross reference you may find is Deuteronomy 7:1-11. Even if it wasn't listed as a cross reference, you would be aware of it if you were reading through the whole book of Deuteronomy (once more, I recommend reading through entire books of the Bible, not just pieces of books). In chapter seven, the Lord warns the Israelites not to be influenced by these nations. The Lord says that the way to avoid their influence is to completely destroy them. This is a matter of life and death for the Israelites, for if they turn from worshiping God, they too will be destroyed (verse 4, below).

1"When the LORD your God brings you into the land you are entering to possess, and He drives out many nations before you — the Hittites, Girgashites, Amorites, Canaanites, Perizzites, Hivites and Jebusites, seven nations more numerous and powerful than you — 2and when the LORD your God delivers them over to you and you defeat them, you must completely destroy them. Make no treaty with them and show them no mercy. 3Do not intermarry with them. Do not give your daughters to their sons or take their daughters for your sons, 4because they will turn your sons away from Me to worship other gods. Then the LORD's anger will burn against you, and He will swiftly destroy you.

5Instead, this is what you are to do to them: tear down their altars, smash their sacred pillars, cut down their Asherah poles, and burn up their carved images. 6For you are a holy people belonging to the LORD your God. The LORD your God has chosen you to be His own possession out of all the peoples on the face of the earth. 7"The LORD was devoted to you and chose you, not because you were more numerous than all peoples, for you were the fewest of all peoples. 8But because the LORD loved you and kept the oath He swore to your fathers, He brought you out with a strong hand and redeemed you from the place of slavery, from the power of Pharaoh king of Egypt.

9Know that Yahweh your God is God, the faithful God who keeps His gracious covenant loyalty for a thousand generations with those who love Him and keep His commands.

10But He directly pays back and destroys those who hate Him. He will not hesitate to directly pay back the one who hates Him. 11So keep the command —

the statutes and ordinances — that I am giving you
to follow today. (Deut 7:1-11, HCSB)

Here we learn that the key issue is the people of Israel are supposed to be a Holy People – people chosen to show a Holy God to the world. The tribes around them are a threat to that holiness, and to the holy relationship they have with God.

So, what have we learned so far? Holiness and sin are very serious issues. The threat of sin and corruption is so great that the people of Israel are to take extreme measures to prevent it. God's holiness is so complete and unalterable that it demands the total destruction of what is not holy.

How then, do these verses show us Jesus? What do they tell us about him, and our relationship with God through him?

First, it shows us our utterly desperate need for God's grace, mercy and forgiveness. If God's demands are so absolute that it demands the killing of the very livestock of sinful people, we have no hope. We need a savior – someone who can take away our sin and give us a holiness that is acceptable to God. In short, we need Jesus Christ; we need his sacrifice on the cross to pay for our sin, and we need his holiness, imparted to us by the Holy Spirit. So, these troubling verses show us our desperate need for Jesus. It shows us what we deserve apart from Jesus – utter annihilation.

Second, if we are already Jesus-followers who have been forgiven and cleansed through his work on our behalf, it teaches us something about living life as his followers. It shows us that sin is very serious. It encourages us to be ruthless toward the sources of sin in our own lives. In fact, it reminds us of what Jesus himself said about being ruthless with sin:

> 29If your right eye causes you to sin, gouge it out and throw it away. For it is better that you lose one of the parts of your body than for your whole body to be thrown into hell. 30And if your right hand causes you to sin, cut it off and throw it away. For it is better that you lose one of the parts of your body than for your whole body to go into hell! (Matt 5:29-30, HCSB)

This all seems pretty helpful. We see that this law, though it is not meant for us to obey literally in this time and place, shows us our sin, our need for a savior, and our need to be ruthless against any source of sin in our own lives.

But I'm sure you still have some questions. What about those poor Canaanite tribes when this law was still in force? They didn't have the option of salvation through faith in Jesus, did they? Let's turn to our Bible-study toolbox and pull out "**scripture interprets scripture**."

First, do we have the right to say that God was wrong to judge the Canaanites in this way?

> 1 So what advantage does the Jew have? Or what is the benefit of circumcision? 2 Considerable in every way. First, they were entrusted with the spoken words of God. 3 What then? If some did not believe, will their unbelief cancel God's faithfulness? 4 Absolutely not! God must be true, even if everyone is a liar, as it is written: **That You may be justified in Your words and triumph when You judge.** 5 But if our unrighteousness highlights God's righteousness, what are we to say? I use a human argument: Is God unrighteous to inflict wrath? 6

> Absolutely not! Otherwise, how will God judge the world? (Rom 3:1-6)

Is God unrighteous to inflict wrath? Absolutely not. His presence destroys sin, whether or not you believe his words.

The Israelites, however imperfectly, were living in faith that God's promises to Abraham were true, and that God would redeem them from their sins. So the Lord included them in what he was *going to do* through Jesus. Their faith in God's promises protected them from God's wrath against sin. The only salvation is through Jesus Christ, by faith. This was true even for the generations who lived before Jesus came. Paul writes to the Romans:

> We are made right with God by placing our faith in Jesus Christ. And this is true for everyone who believes, no matter who we are. For everyone has sinned; we all fall short of God's glorious standard. Yet God, with undeserved kindness, declares that we are righteous. He did this through Christ Jesus when he freed us from the penalty for our sins. For God presented Jesus as the sacrifice for sin. People are made right with God when they believe that Jesus sacrificed his life, shedding his blood. *This sacrifice shows that God was being fair when he held back and did not punish those who sinned in times past, for he was looking ahead and including them in what he would do in this present time.* God did this to demonstrate his righteousness, for he himself is fair and just, and he declares sinners to be right in his sight when they believe in Jesus. (Romans 3:22-26 NLT, emphasis mine)

Everyone in the past who believed God's promises was included in what God was going to do through Jesus. But in Old Testament times, before Jesus had come, those who rejected God became physical illustrations of how serious

God's holiness is, and how big a problem our sin is. God was showing the world their desperate need for a messiah who could bridge the gap between our sin and God's holiness.

In the case of the Canaanite tribes that God commanded Israel to destroy, they were given both a witness to God's holiness and grace, and an abundance of time to repent of sin, and follow God along with the Israelites. From the time of Abraham, to the time of Moses, many hundreds of years passed, in which the Canaanite tribes saw Abraham and his descendants, and how they lived. They saw the people of Israel wandering in the desert for forty years, fed and protected by a loving God. Even so, the Canaanite tribes rejected God's promises, and received the same penalty that ultimately, anyone who rejects God receives. But he gave them many opportunities, over hundreds of years, to have a different future.

I trust you can see how useful the information you have begun to learn can be. It is my hope that when you put into practice what you have discovered in this book, you find that scripture opens up for you, and that even difficult passages of scripture can yield spiritually important messages.

THE POINT:

When we use the tools we have learned in this book, we can gain life-giving insight into the Bible. Even difficult passages can be more clear, and can point us to the grace of God that is given to us through Jesus Christ.

21

A Wonderful Book

Particularly in the beginning of this book, I've made the case that though the Bible is often difficult and confusing, it is worth the effort it takes to understand it. It is historically reliable. It has been faithfully preserved throughout history. Christians believe it is God's Word to us. I've given you some tools to help you see the big picture, and to assist you in getting more out of your Bible reading.

But I want to leave you with one final thought: **You *need* to read the Bible, because it is the foundation and lifeblood of your spiritual existence**.

The Bible is:

<u>The truth that sets us free</u>:

31So Jesus said to the Jews who had believed Him, "If you continue in My word, you really are My disciples. 32You will know the truth, and the truth will set you free." (John 8:31-32, HCSB)

How we receive the Holy Spirit:

2I only want to learn this from you: Did you receive the Spirit by the works of the law or by hearing with faith? (Gal 3:2, HCSB)

A guiding light for how to live:

105Your word is a lamp for my feet and a light on my path. (Ps 119:105, HCSB)

The source of our encouragement and hope:

4For whatever was written in the past was written for our instruction, so that we may have hope through endurance and through the encouragement from the Scriptures. (Rom 15:4, HCSB)

5He established a testimony in Jacob and appointed a law in Israel, which he commanded our fathers to teach to their children, 6that the next generation might know them, the children yet unborn, and arise and tell them to their children, 7so that they should set their hope in God... (Ps 78:5-7, ESV2011)

49Remember Your word to Your servant; You have given me hope through it. (Ps 119:49, HCSB)

Our cleansing:

3You are already clean because of the word I have spoken to you. (John 15:3, HCSB)

17Sanctify them [make them holy] by the truth; Your word is truth. (John 17:17, HCSB)

Our wisdom:

14But as for you, continue in what you have learned and firmly believed. You know those who taught you, 15and you know that from childhood you have known the sacred Scriptures, which are able to give you wisdom for salvation through faith in Christ Jesus. (2Tim 3:14-15, HCSB)

7The instruction of the LORD is perfect, renewing one's life; the testimony of the LORD is trustworthy, making the inexperienced wise. (Ps 19:7, HCSB)

Our comfort:

52LORD, I remember Your judgments from long ago and find comfort. (Ps 119:52, HCSB)

Our Weapon in the Spiritual War:

17Take the helmet of salvation, and the sword of the Spirit, which is God's word. (Eph 6:17, HCSB)

11They conquered him by the blood of the Lamb and by the word of their testimony, for they did not love their lives in the face of death. (Rev 12:11, HCSB)

Our Joy and Delight:

14I rejoice in the way revealed by Your decrees as much as in all riches. 15I will meditate on Your precepts and think about Your ways. 16I will delight in Your statutes; I will not forget Your word. (Ps 119:14-16, HCSB)

111I have Your decrees as a heritage forever; indeed, they are the joy of my heart. (Ps 119:111, HCSB)

Is God's Power for salvation:

16For I am not ashamed of the gospel, because it is God's power for salvation to everyone who believes, first to the Jew, and also to the Greek. 17For in it God's righteousness is revealed from faith to faith, just as it is written... (Rom 1:16-17, HCSB)

14But how can they call on Him they have not believed in? And how can they believe without hearing about Him? (Rom 10:14, HCSB)

Life for us:

45After Moses finished reciting all these words to all Israel, 46he said to them, "Take to heart all these words I am giving as a warning to you today, so that you may command your children to carefully follow all the words of this law. 47For they are not meaningless words to you but they are your life, and by them you will live long in the land you are crossing the Jordan to possess." (Deut 32:45-47, HCSB)

50This is my comfort in my affliction: Your promise has given me life. (Ps 119:50, HCSB)

Here's a pretty good short summary, from Psalm 19:

7The law of the LORD is perfect, reviving the soul;
the testimony of the LORD is sure, making wise the simple;
8the precepts of the LORD are right, rejoicing the heart;
the commandment of the LORD is pure, enlightening the eyes;
9the fear of the LORD is clean, enduring forever;
the rules of the LORD are true, and righteous altogether.
10More to be desired are they than gold, even much fine gold;
sweeter also than honey and drippings of the honeycomb. (Ps 19:7-10, ESV2011)

Imagine there was a food that would make you lose weight, and help you maintain your ideal body weight. Suppose that same food cured cancer, and prevented any new cancer. It would help you sleep well at night, and give you energy during the day. It would help your body regulate your hormones properly, and be a big factor in preventing heart disease. Eating this food would be the best single thing you could do to maintain or gain health. If you ate this food regularly, long term, you would lead a healthy, vigorous life well into your nineties.

Now, there are two catches. The first is that you have to eat this food regularly, and long term, for the health benefits to really kick in. Second, the food has a funny taste. It takes a little getting used to. But there are all sorts of people and books that are available to help you appreciate the strange flavor, and learn to actually enjoy the way it tastes. Millions of people testify that after eating it regularly for a long period, they actually love it.

You struggle with your health in all of the areas helped by this food. But when a friend asks if you eat this miracle-food regularly, you say, "Yeah, I know I probably should, and I do occasionally, but I just can't get over the flavor."

To quote Forrest Gump: "My Momma always says, 'Stupid is as stupid does.'"

Reading the Bible is the single-best thing you can do for your spiritual life and health. Sometimes, at first, it isn't fun or easy. But if you do it *regularly*, and *for the long term*, it will profoundly shape and change your life for the better. It will build up and secure, not your physical health, but the *eternal* health of your very soul. The benefits of reading the Bible far outweigh those of a super-food that will only keep you healthy for ninety years or so.

Far too many people say, "I know I should, and I do occasionally, but I just don't have the time." Or, "...but I just can't get into it," or, "...but it's kind of boring to me."

Once more, I remind you of Forrest Gump's mother. This is foolishness. If you want to be a Christian, you *must* immerse yourself in the Bible. **It is life to you**.

If you are struggling in your life as a Christian, is it possible that at least part of the problem is that you spend very little time reading, learning and soaking in the words of the Bible? If you don't have much peace, or joy or love in your life, could it be that part of the issue is that you are starving yourself spiritually, by not reading the Bible regularly?

Now, I want to make sure you understand, I am not saying that reading the Bible will automatically cure every mental and emotional obstacle you struggle with. Sometimes the Christian life is just difficult. But even then, the Bible encourages us by reminding us that following Jesus does indeed involve suffering and loss, and giving us hope to persevere. And often times, we make it unnecessarily and especially difficult for ourselves, because we do not spend much time or energy dwelling on God's very Word to us.

We have learned where the Bible comes from. We have seen that it is reliable. We have discovered that when we see the big picture, and know a few basic principles for interpreting it, it is understandable. **I encourage you now to see that the Bible is *life* for you.**

My prayer for you is that after reading this book, appreciating, understanding and reading the Bible becomes part of your daily life for the rest of your days.

To God alone be the Glory!

Get Involved!

Did you Enjoy this book?
Would you like to see more like it?
You can help!

In today's world, authors depend upon you, and others like you, to keep telling others about their books.

- If you haven't already, check out Tom Hilpert's other books. He has written both fiction and non-fiction. As of this publication, they include:

  Non-fiction. *In His Image* and *Who Cares about the Bible?*

  Fiction. The Lake Superior Mysteries: *Superior Justice, Superior Storm, Superior Secrets, Superior Getaway* (more to come)

  Young Adult Fantasy Fiction. *The Forgotten King*

- Post about this book (and any of the others), and link to it on Facebook, Twitter, LinkedIN and other social networking sites.

- Review it on Amazon, GoodReads and anywhere else people talk about books. Many of Tom Hilpert's books have a number of positive reviews, but they all came from someone like you, and there is no such thing as too many.
- Tell your friends and family about it. Blog about it.
- Sign up to get emails when new books are released by Tom Hilpert:
  http://eepurl.com/PtO61

Follow Tom Hilpert on Facebook and Twitter (@TomHilpert) Go to his webpage: www.tomhilpert.com, and sign up to receive emails when new books are released. (Or use the link above). His Bible blog is revth.wordpress.com

Acknowledgements

It would be silly to write a book about the Bible without thanking the Ultimate Author, God our Father. To Him be all glory and praise!

I want to also remember and thank Doug Fiehweg for asking me to develop the original sermon series that eventually became the basis for this book. Thanks also to New Joy Fellowship in general for your feedback and questions during the series.

Many thanks to David Sims and Charlotte Ryerson, pre-readers for this book, who both offered a great deal of extremely helpful advice. I always feel bad for my pre-readers, because my books are never as good for them as they are for the rest of my readers, who benefit from their insight. Perhaps someday you'll re-read this, and think, "Boy, that was better than I remembered it." If so, it is because of you.

Once more, as always, thank you to my lovely bride, and partner in all things, Kari Hilpert. Your love and support mean the world to me. Thank you for sparing so much time to my writing endeavors. And for anyone who is still reading this, let it be known that Kari is an excellent copy-editor!

About the Author

 Tom Hilpert grew up in the tropical paradise of Papua New Guinea. When he was ten years old, he knew he wanted to write books. In fact, he began writing several novels at that age. Thankfully, they are lost forever.

However, his more recent works are available in print and eBook formats. His fiction features strong, memorable, quirky characters who face mysteries and adventures with humor and persistence. His non-fiction books are characterized by his ability to put complex concepts into clear, understandable language.

Hilpert has visited more than 17 countries, and has lived in three of them. In the U.S., he has lived in six different states, including Minnesota, the setting for his *Lake Superior Mysteries*. Currently, he lives in Tennessee with his wife, children, and far too many pets and farm animals.

Learn more at http://www.tomhilpert.com
Like Tom's Facebook page here: Tom Hilpert's Facebook Page

APPENDIX A: THE BASIS FOR MODERN TRANSLATIONS

The most recognized Old Testament Hebrew text is called the *Biblia Hebraica Stuttgartensia*. It is in its fifth edition, and almost every version of the Old Testament is translated from it. Many English Bible versions also use the ancient Greek Old Testament (called the Septuagint, abbreviated as "the LXX") and parts of the Dead Sea Scrolls as supplements to help make an accurate, meaningful translation.

The original documents of the New Testament were written in Greek. We have, as I have described, many, many ancient copies of it. But which copy of each book is the best representation of the original documents? There are three main ways that Christians answer this question.

During the middle ages in Europe, scholars switched from Greek to Latin. There are, of course, many ancient Latin copies of the New Testament, but it is not the language in which the apostles wrote. Even so, for many centuries, the only Bible used in Western Europe was the official Latin translation, known as the "Vulgate."

In the sixteenth century, the scholar Erasmus, working with twenty-five ancient Greek manuscripts, assembled one complete Greek text of the New Testament. At the time, he only had access to one copy of the book of Revelation in Greek, and it was missing a part. He had to translate "backwards" from the Latin Vulgate into Greek to complete it. His work was revised several times, and it ended up with the name "*textus receptus*," or "received text." This name came from an introduction that accompanies one of the revisions. Today, there are a number of Christians who say simply, "the *textus receptus* is the only correctly preserved copy of the Greek New Testament." The King James Version is the only English version of the Bible based on the *textus receptus*. However, many more (and better quality) manuscripts have been discovered since the *textus receptus* was formed. Most serious scholars consider the *textus receptus* to be inferior to other available Greek texts. Even so, with that said, we should understand that the differences between the *textus receptus* and the most highly regarded Greek texts are quite insignificant for what Christians believe.

The second approach to forming the best and most accurate representation of the original New Testament is the *majority text*. The majority text was created by compiling all the available readings for each verse, and simply choosing the one found in the largest number of texts (that is, the reading that is found in the *majority* of texts, hence the name). The weakness of this approach is that the older a manuscript is, the less likely it has survived; thus there are larger numbers of later copies. This means that the majority text ends up not taking into account manuscripts that are more ancient (where they are different from the majority) because there are always fewer copies of the older manuscripts. This means that "the majority text" is essentially the same as "the later copies." The New King James Version is based upon the majority text.

The third approach, the one favored by most Bible translators worldwide, is the *critical text*. In the critical text, scholars compare all the ancient manuscripts, just as they do in the majority text. However, the critical text generally favors the oldest available manuscripts, so that if there is a difference, rather than simply picking the majority reading, the critical text gives more weight to readings from older manuscripts.

There are three well-recognized editions of the critical text of the New Testament. The most widely used is called the *Nestle-Aland Novum Testamentum Graece*. It is in its 28th edition, and is sometimes abbreviated to NA28. There are two more critical texts that are almost identical to NA28: the UBS (now in its fifth edition) and the Society for Biblical Literature Greek New Testament (SBLGNT). Translators often use the UBS text or the SBLGNT to help them as they translate, although for the most part, those two are only different from the NA28 in terms of formatting, punctuation and emphasis.

Other than the King James Version and New King James Version, all reputable modern Bible translations are based upon the critical text.

PUTTING IT TOGETHER IN AN EXAMPLE:

To put all this together, imagine that textual scholars are working on Mark 7:8. The critical text has this (translated into English, obviously):

> Disregarding the command of God, you keep the tradition of men." (Mark 7:8, HCSB)

The critical text has this because the *oldest* manuscripts record it as such. However, the *majority* of manuscripts (which means, in essence, the later ones) have it like this (the *textus receptus*, which is also a later text, has the same reading as the majority text in this case):

> Disregarding the command of God, you keep the tradition of men: *the washing of jugs, and cups, and many other similar things you practice.*

The italicized part represents the difference between the critical text and the majority text (and also the *textus receptus*). So a translation based on the majority text would add those words. This is what is known as a "major variant."

I want you to understand two things. First, this doesn't change anything. If you take *out* "the washing of jugs, and cups, and many other similar things you practice," it does not change the meaning of the verse. Or, if you add it *in*, it still does not change the essential meaning of the verse. Once again, what we find is that the text of the New Testament has been accurately preserved, and even among three different textual traditions, the differences are so small as to be meaningless.

Secondly, most Bible translations that are based on the critical text will supply footnotes wherever there is a major variant like this. In other words, a good Bible translation will make sure you can see the small differences between the critical text and the majority text. In this way, even if you don't speak Greek, you can usually see for yourself the most significant differences between the critical text and the majority text.

APPENDIX B: The King James Version

I need to say something about the King James Version (KJV) of the Bible, because if I don't, someone else will. The KJV was the very first English translation that was officially approved by an English-speaking government. The translation was commissioned and approved by King James of England in the year 1611 AD. Some printings of the Bible contain the words "Authorized Version."

I'm not sure why it is, but there is a great deal of ignorance, silliness and misinformation concerning the King James Version of the Bible. It is not hard to meet someone who thinks that the KJV is the only legitimate Bible in English. You might even meet people who think the KJV is more legitimate than the underlying Greek.

Let's start with the silliness and ignorance. Some people point out that it is the only "authorized version." That is true, if they mean it was the only translation of the Bible officially authorized *by King James of England*. However "authorized" does NOT mean: "authorized by *God*."

There are also some folks who seem to think that the KJV is the *original* Bible. They somehow feel that the strange language of the KJV is the language of God. They don't even realize that the original languages were Hebrew, Aramaic and Greek.

About that strange language. The reason for it is that it is generally English *as it was spoken in 1611*. The language has changed a great deal over the past four-hundred years. People read words like "Thee" and "Thou" and imagine that somehow this is meant to convey God's holiness to us. Actually, those words have nothing to do with holiness. Originally, "thee," "thou," and "you," were used in English to indicate whether you were speaking to someone formally, or informally; and whether you were speaking to one person, or more than one person. However, even by 1611, these words were falling into disuse. Certainly today, almost no one recognizes the use of these words in defining number or formality. In any case, those terms have nothing to do with holiness, or even anything religious.

The other strange language, similarly, is not about religion or holiness. It is just *old*. Personally, I think the archaic language has the overall effect of making it seem like the Bible is removed from real life.

Many of the expressions in the KJV sound very beautiful, but they are unnecessarily difficult to understand for modern English speakers. Even many people who prefer the language of the KJV actually do not understand it very well, and often misinterpret Bible verses because of it.

I have read and listened to a number of sermons by preachers who were using the King James Version. Invariably, the preachers had to translate King James English into modern English. This is a very inferior way to teach the Bible, since there are now two translations taking place: one from Greek to KJV English, and then from KJV English to modern language.

There is one argument for the KJV that does deserve some consideration. The KJV is translated from a Greek text popularly called the *textus receptus*, or "received text." That term comes from an introduction to one of the revisions of this text (see more in Appendix A); it does not mean "received from God." The *textus receptus* was widely used for most English Bible translations from the mid-1500s on. In the nineteenth century, however, archaeologists began discovering other copies of the Greek texts, as described in chapter four of this book. Some of the new discoveries were older than the *textus receptus*. Scholars have used all the texts available to them, as well as other archaeological and historical evidence, to compile an extremely accurate Greek New Testament. We call the result of this scholarship "the critical text." There are a number of differences between the *textus receptus* and the critical text.

The more educated "KJV-only" people insist that the *textus receptus* should be the only legitimate Greek text, because, although it had its flaws, discoveries since that time reveal that it is 97% similar to the main body of Greek texts that were used from about 350 AD and on. The argument goes that in the fourth century, the church gathered together this group of Greek texts, deliberately leaving out the other manuscripts which have since been rediscovered and used in the critical text. The idea is that the fourth century church, existing less than three-hundred years after the formation of the New Testament, had a better idea than we do which manuscripts most accurately reflected the originals.

This argument faces a number of challenges. For starters, we don't know for certain which texts were available to the fourth century church. In other words, we don't know that they *deliberately* left out some of the manuscripts used in the critical text today. It may be that those manuscripts were lost *before* the fourth century, and only re-discovered within the past two centuries.

Secondly, although the fourth century was closer to the time of the apostles, archaeology as a scholarly discipline did not really exist at that time. In other words, with almost three hundred years between the fourth century church and the apostles, and no professional archaeologists, they might not have had a good way to know which texts were better. Their decisions could have been based on mistaken traditions.

Third, the *textus receptus* was originally formed without all of the manuscripts that were used in the fourth century. As I pointed out in Appendix A, Erasumus had to "translate backwards" from Latin to Greek to form the earliest copy of the *textus receptus*.

All in all, the use of the textus receptus alone is considered to be inferior in Biblical scholarship. However, let me reiterate what was said in Appendix A. **When all is said and done, the differences between any of the textual traditions is extremely small.** Though the differences between the *textus receptus* and the critical text are numerous, they are also quite minor, **and they do not affect any major doctrine of Christianity**. In other words, in the end, it doesn't actually make much difference whether you use the *textus receptus* or the critical text.

If the critical text really was very different in meaning from the *textus receptus*, then long ago, two branches of Christianity would have developed, based upon the two different textual traditions. That hasn't happened, because the differences are simply not that important.

Of course, all that is for the New Testament. The Hebrew text of the Old Testament is the same for virtually all bibles, which means – again – that the main difference between the KJV and modern translations of the Old Testament, is that the modern translations are much easier to understand.

Made in the USA
Columbia, SC
20 November 2017